Beyond the Postern Gate: A History of Fishergate and Fulford Road

Van Wilson
with additional photography by
Simon I Hill FRPS

Published by the
Archaeological Resource Centre
St Saviourgate, York

with the support of

The Scirebröc Group
and
York Oral History Project

1996

Published by the Archaeological Resource Centre
St Saviourgate, York

12 October 1996

British Library Cataloguing in Publication Data
The Catalogue Record for this book is available from the British Library

ISBN No. 1 874454 13 2

Design and layout is by The Scirebröc Group, York. Tel 01904 672350
Printing is by Quacks, York. Tel 01904 635967

Please note: *for reasons of economy this book has been 'perfect bound'. Breaking the spine of the book will damage the binding and may result in pages becoming separated from the book.*

Cover photograph
Fishergate Postern, from the City Walls, c1900

Inset
Fishergate, c1920

Contents

List of Illustrations

(including source, or photographer, if known)

Foreword

The history of York, from its foundation in AD71 to the present day, has been well documented in many publications. These books, however, are concerned largely with the historic core contained within the medieval walls and the city's relationship with the outside world.

The suburban expansion outside the defences that has resulted in the modern city started at the beginning of the nineteenth century. Decadence was rapidly approaching; the city had lost the role on the national stage which it had enjoyed for many centuries. With road improvements and faster journey times by stage coaches, the gentry who had come to York in the previous century for the cultural and other entertaining events of the season, transferred their allegiance to London. The Corporation's neglect of the River Ouse, an important trading artery, had raised the price of coal and frustrated the growth of industry. The requirement that traders had to be Freemen of the city, limited to one shop each, prevented the development of business. In consequence York's sole role was parasitic, as a market place for its surrounding hinterland and its largest group of workers was in domestic service.

Nevertheless the population, standing at 16,000 at the beginning of the nineteenth century, expanded to 30,000 by 1841, almost entirely due to the migration of countryfolk who, unable to find employment in their own localities, came to York to seek better fortune. Housing immediately outside the walls, was provided for them in Bootham Square, the Groves, Layerthorpe and Nunnery Lane. The Municipal Corporations Act 1835, which converted the city from a self-perpetuating oligarchy into something more nearly approaching a democracy, abolished the privileges of freemen and, with the arrival of the railways in 1839, the conditions for further expansion on a more solid footing were provided. By the end of the century the population had reached 75,812. The twentieth century produced growth of only another 25,000 until the dramatic changes of April 1996 when the contiguous villages were dragged, screaming and bawling in protest, into the new greater York with a population of over 166,000.

Thus in the two decades after 1850 there was almost feverish activity in house building and suburban expansion, an activity that was to continue but at a less frenetic pace for the rest of the century. It was during this period that the communities off Fulford Road were born. Van Wilson, in expanding her earlier history of one of these communities to cover the wider area surrounding Fishergate and Fulford Road, and chronicling its development, has ensured that the lives and activities of the ordinary people of one of York's suburbs are not overlooked and forgotten, something often neglected or only cursorily covered in the larger histories of York.

Hugh Murray
York, 8 September 1996

The History of A Community, Van Wilson, 1984
(A reproduction of the front cover of Van Wilson's earlier work on the history of the Fulford Road district)

Introduction

This book is a revised version of my earlier 'History of a Community: Fulford Road District, York' which was published in 1984. I have expanded the original text to include a wider area, incorporating Fishergate and part of Fulford village. Most of the photographs are new.

Apart from archive material and general directories, there has been no previous work which focuses on Fishergate and Fulford Road. This is partly because the area is not easily categorised, falling between the city of York and the hamlet of Fulford, and is therefore often overlooked. Not being too far from the city itself, it has not really carved out a separate identity, as have many other suburbs. Yet it has a definite life and history of its own, as well as a role to play in the complete history of York. In my research I have used a combination of documentary and oral sources. Although background information has been unearthed from archive documents and newspapers, much of the detail has come from personal interviews with residents and ex-residents of this part of the city.

A hundred and fifty years ago, the area between York and Fulford boasted several lavish houses, set in attractive grounds. Gradually these estates were split up, and together with the nursery land which covered much of Fulford Road, were developed during the 19th century into terraced streets which contain a range of architecture, and their owners a range of occupations. Some streets housed the skilled working classes, whilst others, rather grander in style, were home to the professional middle classes before the mass move to outlying villages. The strong military presence in the form of two barracks; the glassworks; the cattle market in nearby Paragon Street; and the river as a means of transport, have together ensured plenty of employment.

In more recent years the area has moved away in some measure from its roots, and become less clearly defined in terms of class. It has undergone many changes from the time of its widespread development - in its physical appearance, in its adaptation of the buildings and institutions, and in the personal and family lives of its inhabitants. There have been suggestions that any sense of community has long since disappeared. This is true, of course, in many big cities where terraced streets have been demolished and replaced by blocks of high-rise flats, which deprive their occupants of the friendly and close-knit atmosphere which they had once known. But I would suggest that this area has remained constant. It refutes the view that such communities have vanished totally, because, despite the changes, there is a 'community spirit' which still exists.

I would like to thank all those people whose history I feel privileged to share. I do not pretend that this work is a totally comprehensive one, for the history of any area is constantly changing. Above all it is a history of people, and therefore that history is a continuing one.

Van Wilson
York, 12 October 1996

Acknowledgements for the First Edition 1984

I would particularly like to thank Ken and Winnie Richmond who first suggested the idea of a history of this area, and for their help and information. I should also like to thank the following, who shared with me their personal memories, lent photographs, and gave access to deeds and family papers:

Norma Barker, Ian Beilby, Gwen Benson, Pauline Bridge, Ron Burnett, the late Brian Caffrey, Mr T Chilton, the late Mr & Mrs F Crawford, Mr Len & Mrs Nancy Dawson, the late Ernest Driffield, Florence Fenn, Millie Fenn, Ms M Holliday, George Kent, Geoff Lee, Mary Lewis, Roy Luxton,

May Molloy, Mr H Morgan, Mrs Peavey, the late Keith Raw, Mr & Mrs John Shannon, Ron Sheppeard, Miss E M Slyth, Mrs Sollitt, John Taylor.

I wish to thank the following for answering specific queries or for giving access to official documents: Bass North Breweries; the late David Black - Royal Commission on Historical Monuments; the staff of the Borthwick Institute of Historical Research; the late Irene Briddon; Colonel R K Cooley of Imphal Barracks; Brigadier Malcolm Cubiss - Regimental HQ of Prince of Wales' Own Regiment; Peter Dalton - ex-landlord of Wellington Inn; Mike Dickinson - Planning Department, City Council; Inspector George Duck; Mr M Fielding - Estate Surveyors, Catterick; John Hatfield - Wills & Probate Sub-Registry; Pat Hendry - Holly Croft Social Services Department; John Hirst - Catholic Housing Aid Society; Joseph Kershaw - ex-landlord of the Fulford Arms and Karel Tripp - Estates Department, City Council.

I should like to thank, for their advice and guidance in the early stages of this work: Jill Freeman of the Ripon Community History Project, Dr Greg Lodge of the University College of Ripon and York St John and Bob Poole of the York Oral History Project.

Special thanks are due to Rita Freedman and Mary Thallon of the York City Archives for suggestions and advice, and for giving me access to various documents. Quotations from this material are with the permission of York City Archives Ltd.

I am grateful for permission to quote from articles in both the Yorkshire Gazette and Yorkshire Evening Press, to Cambridge University Press for permission to quote from Frances Finnegan's 'Poverty and Prostitution : A Study of Victorian Prostitutes in York', and to Hugh Murray for permission to quote from his book 'Horse Tramways of York 1880-1909'. I am also grateful for the help given by the staff of York Reference Library, and to Maurice Smith for permission to quote from material in the York History Room, to the Building Control Department of the City Council

for access to plans, to Tom Roberts of the Institute of Advanced Architectural Studies for architectural information, and to John Worrallo and the late Lawrie Watson for photographic reproduction.
I should like to thank Mrs Brinning and staff of the Archives Department in Beverley for access to documents relating to the East Riding; Rita Biggins for assistance in my research; and Rev David Reynolds, formerly vicar of St Oswald's Church, Fulford, for providing access to church documents, and allowing me to quote freely from Fulford Parish Magazines.

Special thanks are due to Chris Clay of University College of Ripon and York St John for his encouragement, support and advice, and to Dr Ian Gibbs of the University of York for his help and advice in the process of editing and printing. I should also like to thank Roy Stevens who read the manuscript of the first edition and made useful suggestions.

Acknowledgements for this edition 1996

I would like to thank York Oral History Project for their support of this publication and the following people, whose oral testimonies appear for the first time in this edition:

The late Walter Atkin, Frederick Atkinson, Noel Attree, Eileen Brown, Mr and Mrs Ray Close, Josie Cooper, Mr Francis, Claire Graham, Terry Kilmartin, Gertrude Levi, June Lloyd-Jones, Helen McTurk (nee Wildon), Annie Pinder, Tom Rhodes, Betty Thompson, Andy Waudby and one or two others who wish to remain anonymous.

I wish to thank Dr Andrew 'Bone' Jones, Director of the ARC, for his support; Mr Brian Atkin for information about the Sisters of Charity of St Vincent de Paul; Margaret Bracegirdle, for sharing with me the results of her research on the Grange Estate, and the loan of photographs; Howard and Annie Dickenson for information about Marlborough Villas; Brian

Hardyman for information about the glassworks and glassmaking; Frances Mee, Editor at York Archaeological Trust, for her meticulous reading of the text and her many useful suggestions; Joe Murphy for the loan of photographs; David Poole for information on Lord Mayors, centenarians and York cemetery, and for assisting with my research; Mike Race of the York Oral History Project for material on pubs, for reading the first draft of the text and making useful comments, and for assisting with my research; and Ken Shelton for his information about New Walk Terrace and the loan of photographs.

I would like to thank Hugh Murray, for information on the Soldier's Home, the loan of several photographs, for reading the manuscript and making useful suggestions, and for kindly agreeing to write the Foreword to this book. I am also indebted once again to Simon I Hill for his excellent modern photography and reproduction of old pictures, to The Scirebröc Group for their financial and practical support of the work, and to the Sheldon Memorial Trust for their award of a grant to this project.

Last but not least, my thanks are due to Peter Wilson for his encouragement and support, and to my children, Philippa and Toby, whose humour and love keep me sane.

Dedicated to Peter, Philippa and Toby

Fishergate Postern, 1996

1

Street of the Fishermen

Fishergate (the street of the Fishermen) originally started from George Street (off Walmgate) and continued out through Fishergate Bar, one of the exits (the other being Walmgate Bar) from the city towards Fulford. The street was recorded as early as 1070, when it was known as Fiscergate.

Fishergate Postern, c1900

A walk along Fishergate today would begin at Fishergate Postern, which stands at the foot of Piccadilly, and is the only one of York's posterns to remain unaltered, with a gateway at the side. Any history of this part of

York must start from the postern gate. The postern once stood right beside the Foss, so that it would often emerge out of the water, as this part of the King's fish pool was permanently flooded. On the first floor was a projecting lavatory which issued straight out into the waters below. The farmhouse style roof is of the 17th century. At the beginning of the 19th century, the postern housed a white and red lead manufacturers.

Castle Mills Bridge links Tower Street with the approach to Fishergate and has its wharf in Browney Dyke. In the lock, several barges can usually be seen, including two from Acaster Transport who hold the contract for bringing paper from Goole to the wharf at Wormald's Cut behind the Yorkshire Evening Press in Walmgate. These are the last examples of river traffic in the city, which once saw many such vessels at work. In 1888 the locks were altered to allow larger vessels to pass through to Leethams flour mills. One of the stand-by barges, originally a sand dredger which helped to clean the Ouse and Foss canals, was called Reklaw, which is Walker spelt backwards (as Walker's coal company in Layerthorpe owned the barges). This particular barge was restored and refurbished in March 1996, as a result of a challenge by Minster FM Radio and the York Advertiser. Many volunteers came forward to help with the project and local businesses funded the repair and maintenance of the barge, which is primarily to be used to provide river trips for the disabled, though other groups can hire the vessel. There are eight berths, a kitchen and bathroom and full facilities for disabled people, including a hydraulic wheelchair lift.

At the beginning of this century, the lock-keeper for Castle Mills lived at Number 1 Fishergate, and opposite him were Phoenix House, which housed a chicory merchant and a brick and tile manufacturer, and the neighbouring Phoenix Cottage. Mrs Gertrude Levi remembers as a child at the turn of the century driving over Castle Mills Bridge with her father, and witnessing a very sad scene,

There used to be a man sat at the top of the steps where you go down to that lock. And he didn't have any hands, what he had was two square pieces of wood with carpet on the bottom. He seemed to be sitting on his legs and his eyes used to go rather peculiar as well. And many times when we used to be driving, I knew that man would be there selling boxes of matches, and as soon as we were approaching the bridge, I used to turn my head away because I was so upset.

Also situated on Castle Mills Bridge was a steam marble works. By the 1840s, the Waudby family (related to the Waudbys who had the fish business in Fossgate) were owners of the works. John Waudby retired in 1846 and was succeeded by his sons Charles and Joseph. It is very likely that the steam engine, which the company owned, was used for cutting the stone. This would have considerably shortened the time spent on production.

According to the York Cemetery cash books, men were paid by the foot for piece work, to saw different stone and marble. They could command fourpence-halfpenny per foot, which worked out at quite a good wage. Much of their work would be on door lintels and fireplaces for the middle classes, but the cemetery would also need their services. Despite this, the marble works went bankrupt in 1856, and George Jennings, who had worked for the Waudbys, opened a steam marble mill in Piccadilly.

The Castle Mills works did start up again, however, because there is an advertisement in the York Directory of 1881, for Joseph Thistlethwaite, Steam Marble Works. The advert reads 'J. Thistlethwaite, Monumental Sculptor and Marble Mason begs to inform the Nobility and Architects of York and vicinity that he has commenced business on his own account at the above premises, where he intends to carry on the business in all its branches. All Work executed by practical workmen under J T's own superintendence'.

In 1881, Joseph Morton, cabinet maker and undertaker of Frances Street, had his workshops on Castle Mills Bridge. Today this corner of the bridge, opposite the postern, is the home of a garage, originally Oxtoby's, which was founded in 1922 by brothers Tom and Richard Oxtoby. After Richard's death in 1955, the business was modernised, and a new showroom opened in 1958, with a car wash added in 1962. In 1975 it was bought by the Tyke Petroleum Company.

This part of the bar walls from the Postern round towards Fishergate Bar, restored in 1345, is very attractive in Spring, when it is adorned with a carpet of yellow daffodils. The Bar was known in the 14th century as St George's Bar. It was certainly a substantial entrance-way, with a superstructure, portcullis, and possibly even a barbican. In 1489 heavy taxation by Henry VII led to riots and both the nearby Walmgate Bar and this bar were severely damaged by fire; scorch marks are still visible here. The gateway was afterwards bricked up and in the 16th century the tower housed a prison or House of Correction, with appalling conditions. Many inmates were even suffering from the plague. One of the towers in the Bar was occupied by prostitutes. Another part was also reputedly York's first lunatic asylum, where people were vermin-ridden and regularly beaten.

In 1827 when the Cattle Market was established in Fawcett Street, the bar was re-opened for cattle to be driven through, and as the ground nearby was cleared, human remains were discovered, probably victims of the plague. The bar was restored in 1961, and the City Arms above renewed. Today there is only access for pedestrians and cyclists, and three bollards prevent any cars coming through. One rarely sees a cow in the vicinity now!

In the part of Fishergate just within the bar, was the Cordwainers' (shoemakers') Maison Dieu, a kind of almshouse, which was founded in 1436. In 1548 there were five men residing there, and they received an annual pension of one shilling each. The last remains of the building were gone by 1936.

Fishergate Bar, 1996

Funeral of Lord Mayor, 4 February 1907

Today Fishergate is a busy thoroughfare, being one of the main roads into the city from the A19, which also connects with the A64 bypass, and traffic is heavy at most times of the year. In the 19th and early 20th century, the road was often the scene of military parades and processions. Cavalrymen would ride back to the barracks, in all their finery, and when Military Sunday (see chapter 4) began, Fishergate was thronged with expectant crowds.

On 4th February 1907, the funeral of the 53 year old Lord Mayor, William Bentley, took place, and the coffin was escorted by troops from the 18th Hussars, West Yorkshires, and the Yorkshire and Lancashire Regiment along this route. Bentley was a well-loved figure in the city, although he had only been elected as Mayor in the previous November, and was one of only three Mayors in modern times to die in office. His term of office was completed by Samuel Border, the provision merchant whose store was in Coney Street, and who stepped in, having previously been Lord Mayor, and therefore 'knew the ropes'. Bentley had been Sheriff twice whilst living at Fulford Grange (1903-1905), as well as a magistrate, and was instrumental in raising funds for York County Hospital. He is commemorated by a marble bust in York Guildhall.

This stretch of Fishergate now houses a variety of businesses including a chop suey house, antiques shop, gent's hairdresser, shoe repairer, bookmaker's, reflexology centre and, most recently, a Caribbean restaurant. The attractive original frontage of Oxtoby's painters and decorators stands out in this row. The firm was established in 1889 by Thomas Metcalfe Oxtoby, and continued as a family-run business. Unfortunately, the eldest son (who had joined the Royal Scots) was reported missing and later killed in 1917. On Thomas's death in 1933, his other sons Dan and Frank took over until their retirement in the 1970s, when the business was sold to a Leeds-based group. It was bought back in 1983 by Rod Oxtoby, T.M.'s grandson, but it went into liquidation in 1993. Today the name remains, but the shop sells pine furniture.

In 1900, these shops were rather more mundane, and included two tobacconists, two bootmakers, a costumier, two confectioners, a butcher, a newsagent, and Avisons photographer (a name which can still be spotted on the back of old studio photos from this period). But in 1876 the city nuisance inspector operated from number 10, and in 1893 there was a chemist's shop along here, owned by Robert Whisker, who advertised Whisker's Nursery Hair Lotion as 'a boon to mothers' because it was 'harmless and non-greasy' and highly recommended for 'expelling nits and parasites'.

Terry Kilmartin remembers the barbers' in this row of shops,

Mr Sanderson was in Walmgate and they moved to Fishergate. His son was a prisoner of war, he learnt to barber there, and came back and took the shop. After the war you used to go to Sandy's for a haircut 'down to the wood'.

On the corner of Paragon Street and Fishergate are the Festival Flats, built in 1951 for the Festival of Britain. These flats were one of two prize-winning blocks in the city, the others being in Castlegate. Their little railed balconies were considered to be very elegant. Number 53 Fishergate, just before the Edinburgh Arms, was the home in 1881 of a Frenchman, Augustus Claude Gaget, who had fought in the Franco-Prussian war. In 1878 he came to England and married an Englishwoman in London, but gave French names to his four children, Augustine, Francois, Leon and Emile. He came to York as a commercial traveller, met up with Joseph Rowntree and in 1879 joined Rowntrees Cocoa Works to take charge of the French confectionery department. Gaget introduced several different kinds of sweets, including Almond Paste, and he developed the production of clear gums and fruit pastilles. By 1891 he had left Fishergate to move to Union Terrace and finally died in 1906 at the age of 62.

Another native of France, as well as a centenarian, also lived in Fishergate, quite near to Gaget. This was Louise Lacamp, who was the

St Louis Preparatory School, 1996

principal of the St Louis preparatory school at 7 Marlborough Grove from 1935 to 1969, being assisted by her sister Madeleine. Louise's father Edouard Lacamp, a Free Frenchman, had come to York from Eastbourne in 1911 to be chef at the Royal Station Hotel. The family attended St George's Catholic Church and Louise became a Conservative city councillor, from 1952 to 1967. She died in 1988 at the age of 103.

Just past the flats, on the corner of a short lane, once the other half of Kent Street, is a butchers' shop. On the 1891 Ordnance Survey map, this is clearly the original site of the Edinburgh Arms. The pub is now at the other side of the snickelway, on the site of a lavish building Fishergate Villa. In 1873 two Fishergate Villas were offered for sale, this one being the home of William Wilkinson Wilberforce, later Mayor. It was a good sized house, with garden, coach house and saddle room, as well as a number of trees and shrubs, a greenhouse and vinery. The major attraction was a lovely iron water fountain, which had been bought at an exhibition in 1862. The villa backed onto Cattle Market Road, now Fawcett Street. It was offered for sale again in 1892, and in 1907 Ronald Gray the piano manufacturer lived at the Villa. The villa on the corner of Fishergate and Fawcett Street, a smaller house, was also known as Fishergate Villa, and was built in the early part of the 19th century. In 1873 it was occupied by Captain Cave. It only had four bedrooms rather than the six in the larger villa, but it did have servants' attics, dressing rooms, and two kitchens, though no nursery is mentioned. The garden had ornamental trees and shrubs, but no fountain like its sister property. This is the house now known as Ivy Cottage, a guesthouse with attractive red latticed windows.

In 1881, there is mention of Ivy Villa, which is more than likely this same house. It was the home of T.H. Harmon, Professor of Dancing and Drill Master, who held daily classes for students of varying ages.

Between the two villas is another interesting building, at Number 29. Built in the late 18th century, it was acquired in the late 19th century by the Sisters of Charity of St Vincent de Paul. St Vincent de Paul was a French priest who founded the order of the Vincentian Fathers, and with the help of St Louise de Marillac, founded the Congregation of the Daughters of Charity in Paris in 1633. At the very beginning and again in later years, the nuns were called the Daughters of Charity, yet are still referred to as the Sisters.

Ivy Cottage, 1996

The Old Convent, 1996

Their order came to York in approximately 1888, residing initially at Number 24 George Street, being attached to St George's Catholic Church. They were introduced into York by Lord Ralph and Lady Kerr. Not to be confused with the order of the Sisters of Charity of St Paul, who worked at St Wilfrid's Church, these sisters were a teaching order, but also visited the sick and poor.

As their work grew, they began to look for bigger premises, so moved to Fishergate in 1890. They were able to run evening classes and clubs for young boys and girls, as well as a social club for mothers. There was a large room downstairs, used as a visiting room, a good-sized kitchen, and upstairs was the chapel. The nuns also had their own private quarters. In 1902 a large wing was added for a day nursery. The interior is certainly rather splendid, with a staircase window glazed with flashed coloured quarries. On the top storey is a dummy window, painted in white, and the back gate still bears the sign 'The Old Convent'.

Mike Race, an ex-pupil of St George's school, remembers the nuns,

They were quite striking in their appearance. They used to have this large hat, which had two great wings, and this starched front above a long blue dress, a white starched front which went across the front of them, and a long blue dress which went to the floor and must have had any number of petticoats under it. I often used to think they must have struggled on a windy day, the wind must have caused them great problems with their hats.

The Sisters' work was split between teaching and social work. Terry Kilmartin remembers the nuns teaching at St George's Primary School, which they did from the beginning of this century until 1985,

They were hard but fair, good at giving t'cane, but they fetched some good pupils out of there.

Mr Brian Atkin was a friend of the Sisters and recalls,

Besides teaching, their other specific duty was to help within the parish, primarily visiting. Not only St George's parish, they also provided a visiting sister for St Aelred's, and in later years, a visiting sister for St Margaret Clitherow's. Each sister used to have a little book, which she'd pass on to the other sisters if she left. So they'd know who to visit and where they lived.

They used to run sewing classes for the mums and they used to hold meetings there. The down-and-outs used to call in for a cup of soup and a piece of bread.

The nuns looked after some children whose mothers went out to work, like Mrs Annie Pinder, whose mother had to go potato picking,

The nuns was very good to you, they used to mebbe take you down. You know them aspidistra plants, you could sponge 'em down and they'd give you cocoa. It had a nursery there, and you could take your children in if these women was going in the fields to work. They could take their children in before they went to work and pick 'em up when they come out and I think it was about fourpence.

The Sisters also had other jobs in the parish, as Mr Atkin points out,

For many years Sister Magdalen looked after the church. I suppose you'd call her the sacristan. She used to arrange flowers for the altar when there were weddings and suchlike, and when it was coming up to Christmas and she used to organise helping the church cleaners to make sure the church was clean. She did that for many years. She came to York in '56 I think it was, she must have done it for about 30 years.

When the nuns eventually retired from their paid work, there was still plenty of other work to do. They would visit old people's centres such as Holly Croft and Willow House, and would become involved in Third World Projects. Others worked closely with children, including Sister

Frances who had previously worked in a mother and baby unit in Manchester.

Mr Atkin explains,

You don't retire as a nun, you just get another job. They did marvellous work. They were very missed, and still are. Especially when a tragedy happens, they would go round to the house and visit people, be sympathetic and counsel and console people.

In 1972 the Sisters left Fishergate and moved to a smaller house in Lawrence Street. By the mid-eighties they had left York. The last sisters were Sister Magdalen and Sister Mary, who was last Headmistress of St George's Primary School. The old convent was transformed into flats. Many of these were occupied by young single business people, including trainee managers for Marks and Spencers, and other people working for Radio York when it was first set up.

As early as 1925, the Parish bought a plot in York Cemetery for the Sisters of Charity. The plinth with cross above (recently broken by vandals but, thankfully, now replaced), is dedicated to the memory of seven ladies - Sister Teresa Brett, who died in 1925 after 26 years of religious vocation; Sister Teresa Tonge, who died in 1945 with a vocation of 42 years; Sister Louise Cushion, who died in 1957 with a vocation of 62 years; Sister Agnes Grogan who died in 1975 with a vocation of 54 years; Sister Gerard Hannigan who died in 1967 with a vocation of 47 years; and the Sisters' housekeeper, Catherine Hagan, who died in 1982 in her 100th year, after devoting 40 years to looking after the Sisters. Sister Philomena Manachan is also remembered on the monument, although she is interred at Darlington, following her death in 1922, after 21 years of vocation.

The Society of St Vincent de Paul (SVP) was founded in 1833 by a student, Frederic Ozanam, and some companions. It is 'dedicated to alleviating all forms of poverty, through personal contact and friendship, regardless of race, creed or ideology'. St Vincent de Paul was chosen as patron saint because of his works of mercy and love of the poor. Although the order is no longer in this city, the Society (attached to St George's Church) flourishes. Terry Kilmartin is one of the members,

I mean they've allus looked after the old people. The SVP did 1300 visits last year, that's in the parish. And everybody's looked after who has financial difficulties. In fact they've started a campaign at back o't'church now, everybody takes food in and requesting tins of this and that and the other, and sugar and bread and all like that. They're feeding the five thousand that come knocking at the door and also feeding old people and people who's got in difficulties, young couples. And they've got computer working on it, even sorting all t'old people's names out. And if anyone goes in hospital, they follow 'em up to see how they are.

We run a trip to Bridlington next month. Take two busloads, we're taking the old people this time. But we do stalls for the handicapped, and blind, which is at Holme-on-Spalding-Moor.

This section of Fishergate, where it meets Fulford Road, was named High Fishergate in the late 19th century. In 1881, at number 18, was Dodd's Cab, Carriage and Dog Cart Establishment. They advertised 'waggonettes, landaus and flys on very moderate terms', and 'weddings conducted in good style'.

On the other side of the road, just past the top of Blue Bridge Lane, is a grand house set back a little from the road. This is Fishergate House, built as a family residence for the owner Thomas Laycock in 1837 and designed by the Atkinson brothers, John and William, at a cost of £4,500. Like Brierley with schools, the Atkinsons had their own specialist area - the rebuilding and restoration of York churches, including St Helen's, St Mary Bishophill Junior and Senior, Holy Trinity Micklegate and St Clement's on Scarcroft Road. The design of this house with its impressive Ionic porches was influenced by Sir John Soane. The house had five acres of ornamental pleasure grounds, gardens and a paddock, with a greenhouse and small cottage suitable for a gardener. The building itself comprised a hall, drawing room, dining room, library, breakfast room, servants' hall, butler's pantry, housekeeper's room, kitchen and office on the ground floor. Upstairs were five best bedrooms and three others, dressing rooms, servants' bedrooms, and three water closets. Outside were the usual stables and coach house. In 1847 Laycock died, and left the property to his wife Elizabeth. She herself died in 1859, leaving the house to her daughters Maria and Eliza. In 1868 the two ladies sold the property to Ambrose Walker for £3150. The indenture stated that the mansion was erected on the site of a previous 'messuage or dwelling-house in the occupation of John Tweedy Esq'.

Fishergate House, 1996

Walker sold part of the estate in July 1874 to two York booksellers, John Cooper Chapman and Edward Pickering for £2500. This included an agreement that the property could not be used for glassworks, pot manufactory, forge smith's shop or any noisy or offensive trade. No steam engine could be used on the land, and no public house, alehouse or tavern could be erected.

By 1880 the house itself had become the Girls' Public Day School, with Miss Clark as headmistress. The school moved to High Petergate in 1900, and in 1931 Fishergate House was taken over by the army. Throughout the war it housed the Royal Engineers, civilians and army personnel. On the wall outside is a stone marking WD1, the war department boundary. The house became a listed building in 1980, and was bought for £135,000 as a subsidiary of Shepherd Building Group. Today there is little evidence of the earlier grandeur of the mansion and its beautiful surroundings. The front garden is overgrown and full of weeds, and the house is shabby and gloomy.

Arcading on Fulford Road

Among the more interesting and rather incongruous sights along Fishergate, is the arcading outside the Saxon House Hotel. This is part of John Harper's original arcading, made of magnesian limestone, from the Theatre Royal in St Leonard's Place. Although it is in the Elizabethan style, it was actually only built in 1834. When the Theatre had a brand new Gothic frontage, in 1880, decorated with carved heads of Shakespearean heroines (Lady Macbeth, Cleopatra and Titania) beside Queen Elizabeth I, this arcading was moved to a private residence on Fulford Road called Chelmsford House. Only three of the eight arches remain outside the Saxon Hotel, as well as a smaller part a few yards further along, and another section in the grounds of the Priory Hotel. After Chelmsford House was demolished, the arches fronted a warehouse, bicycle store and now a day nursery. The stretch of terrace still bears the sign of Chelmsford Place. Mrs Gertrude Levi was born in the Place in 1897 and lived there for some years,

I think the first outstanding thing I remember was my father bringing me downstairs to see a lot of the soldiers marching past our house and for the very first time I saw them in khaki and these sort of helmets that I hadn't seen. I'd always seen them coming down Fulford Road in all their lovely scarlet jackets and their full dress uniforms, both Cavalry and Infantry, which were very beautiful to me. I felt really terrified seeing all these men passing so close to our house. It was midnight and I'd never been brought downstairs before. They were coming back from the Boer War, it would have been 1901 or 1902.

Her father was in business in Chelmsford Place as a fruiterer and florist, and the family also had gardens on Osbaldwick Lane. He had begun his career working for Backhouse's, and became well-known in his field, winning prizes for his vegetables and chrysanthemums. She recalls going with him in the pony and trap to make deliveries,

Sometimes it was very nice going to the Cavalry Barracks because all these men, the cooks and the staff sergeant, used to see to the food, and they always used to

give me dainty little bits. Trifles and lovely things out of the kitchen. We used to supply them with vegetables and fruit.

Opposite the arcading, and almost next to Fulford Grange (see chapter 2), is the Priory Hotel. This was once the Rectory of St Margaret's Church in Walmgate, three quarters of a mile away, and is described in 'Within the City Walls', a vivid account of the happy childhood of the rector's daughter, Margaret Mann Phillips. Her father, the Rev Francis Mann, was Rector from 1909 to 1929 and Mrs Phillips tells of how her father would often give away his clothes, to any poor person who called at the Rectory. He could not bear to turn anyone away. In 1929 the family left York, when the Rector accepted the living of Stainton-in-Cleveland. Margaret Mann Phillips went on to graduate from Somerville College, Oxford, and then in 1934 completed a doctorate at the University of Paris, with her thesis on Erasmus. Her brother Reverend Francis John Mann became curate at St Clement's Church.

Priory Hotel, 1996

The front of the hotel is very attractive, with its ivy-covered front wall, and an imitation Dutch step-gable and two round portholes in the attic resembling eyes. The piece of arcading in the garden looks like a mock medieval ruin and to come upon this lovely scene is like a step back in time. During the First World War, the Rector offered to entertain groups of soldiers to meals each Thursday evening. They came to enjoy those visits, not just for the food, but the company and the singing, which helped to make them feel at home. According to maps of the 1920s, the house may well have been divided into two, the Priory and the Rectory, but is now one building again, as the Hotel.

Arcading in garden of Priory Hotel, 1996

At the junction of Fulford Road and Cemetery Road is the Fulford Conservative Club, built in 1810. On the wall above is a cast-iron support jutting out which must have belonged to the overhead tramlines, though it is probably a replacement rather than the original.

A new terrace, rather more up-market in its Regency design, began to appear off Fishergate in 1825. This was New Walk Terrace, on the edge of the Grange estate. Part of the terrace replaced the former Lady Well Close, according to the Victoria County History of York. The Close surrounded the Lady Well, and was advertised in the York Courant of April 1749,

Junction of Fishergate and Cemetery Road, c1920

"The cold bath called the Lady Well adjoining the New Walk is now opened for the summer season, where proper persons will constantly attend upon such ladies and gentlemen as intend to bath. The dwelling houses and close adjoining the well are to be let separately or together."

The charge for bathing was threepence, including the use of a towel, but a penny each for any extra towels. In 1745 the Michaelmas Quarter

Sessions had heard the case of John Roberts, who had stolen two pairs of worsted stockings from the Lady Well House. He was found guilty of 'feloniously stealing and carrying away' the stockings 'against the peace of our Sovereign Lord the King, his crown and dignitary'.

The new owner in August 1845 was Mark Harbert. He advertised in the Yorkshire Gazette,

"The water has long been celebrated for its purity. Ladies and Gentlemen wishing to drink of it may be supplied from a spring in the garden, by applying at the cottage."

After an analysis of water in the Ouse and Foss from two wells and nineteen pumps in the city, Joseph Spence concluded that the purest proved to be "Ouse water from pumps at Museum, Asylum, Layerthorpe Bridge and Lady Well on New Walk".

New Walk Terrace, 1910

Ten residents lived in New Walk Terrace in 1830 including the bath keeper, Isaac Hodgson, and two new houses were advertised in 1831. Another eight were built in 1836. In May 1847, five more newly erected 'genteel dwelling houses' were offered for sale. Each one included gardens, coach house, stable and outbuildings, and 'commanded a beautiful view of the surrounding country and the river to Ouse Bridge'. This block of houses are now at the bottom of the terrace. Many are distinguished by the Dutch bell-gables, and in number 17 there can be seen a small cannon in the garden, a replica similar to the ones which were situated on Blue Bridge. This was bought in Leeds several years ago by the previous owner, Neville England.

Cannon in New Walk Terrace, 1996

On the 1851 census, there is a record of Richard Kirk, the New Walk policeman, living next door to the Bath House. In 1869, Ambrose Walker designed two more houses, and he and his brother, John, worked on more in 1878. By 1893 there were 31 houses. At number 29 the Chief Constable, George Whitfield, lived, and between numbers 12 and 13 was a school. There is a lane between those two houses today, and numbers 12a and 12b look as if they have been built into the gap. There are rising suns set in stained glass in the upstairs windows, and each one has a garden full of hydrangea bushes, with attractive fences dividing them, a touch of leafy suburbia. Down the lane, at the rear of the houses, can be seen the remains of a schoolroom. This was the Melbourne House Private School, at number 12 in 1898. There have been at least three other schools in the Terrace. The garden at number 15 still has a stone bearing the notice '1871 Boys' School', and in the 1970s the Wentworth Nursery School was based at number 6. Around the turn of the century, there was a school run by the Wilkinsons at number 3. Mrs Levi was a pupil there,

I went to a private school, Miss Wilkinson. Then she and her sister had to go to live in Harrogate because the doctor said it was too near the river for her and she sold out to two young ladies. One was the music teacher, the other the school teacher. There were thirty children and when we moved, I should think there were forty of us. That was my education, I never went to a Board school. It was very homely and the children were all very nice. They soon put me at my ease.

Over the next few years, the street housed members of the middle classes. Bank managers, engineer's managers, surveyors, architects, and garrison masters, were amongst the occupations represented. Henry Rhodes Brown, father of the founder of W P Brown's store, ex-Blue Coat School boy and one time Lord Mayor lived at number 12 in 1898, next door to the school. A few years earlier there was a gentleman living in the terrace with the unusual Christian name of Blackader (spelt with one d)!

The street is one of the few which boasts three types of architecture in one terrace - Regency, Victorian and mid-20th century.

In 1881, part of the Fishergate House estate was developed for housing, creating Osborne Terrace, six houses facing the river at the foot of Marlborough Grove. These were built by John Lee (see chapter 3). The Abstract of Title of 1883 for one of these houses refers to ground adjoining New Walk, in 'the newly formed street called Marlborough Grove'. By the beginning of this century, Osborne Terrace had been renamed Marlborough Villas. One of the villas has a blue metal plaque on the outside wall, with the letters BDC on it, inside what resembles a steering wheel. The owners believe this to stand for Bentley Driver's Club, but investigation as to its origin is continuing.

BDC Plaque, Marlborough Villas, 1996

By 1893 Marlborough Grove had twelve houses. At the top of the street, outside the video store Movie World, is a pillar box with the initials VR on the front, one of the few Victorian post boxes left in York, and quite incongruous to be found beside such an example of modern 20th century life.

Melbourne Street on the other side of Fulford Road was built in the 1860s, with part of the street being called Melbourne Terrace before the turn of the century. Hence the name of the Wesleyan Chapel at the junction with Cemetery Road, Melbourne Terrace Methodist Church. The street originally housed the skilled working classes. In the early 1980s, the old church was pulled down. It had been on the line of a proposed inner ring road, so in view of this, it was allowed to deteriorate. Severe gales finally finished it off. In September 1986 a brand new church (designed by the architect Ian Shuttleworth) was opened, with a special ceremony, and a former member, Rev Geoffrey Chatterton, was the preacher.

Fishergate, c1920s

2

Fulford Grange

At the entrance to Grange Garth today, one can see a delightful cottage, considered to be one of York's prettiest houses. It was built in 1835 as the Lodge to the Fulford Grange estate. The little white fence in front is reminiscent of a rural railway signalman's cottage, and a part of the original railings can still be seen in the bushes, though the front gates are much newer.

The original estate consisted of the Grange itself, the Gardener's Cottage, and the Lodge, together with stables, barns, outbuildings and open land formerly part of Lady Well Close.

The Grange is a late Regency building of 1830 to 1840, which includes an 18th century section. The Victoria County History of York states that Fulford Grange had been built by 1794. It has been home to several prominent York merchants. John Maude, the tea-dealer, owned premises in High Ousegate and a town house, as well as Fulford Grange in the 1790s. His two children were baptised in Fulford church and he died in 1796. His son became a captain in the Royal Navy and was instrumental in seizing several loads of smugglers' cargo from Yarmouth in the 1780s. He also commanded the 'Leopard', the same ship as Jane Austen's brother, Frank.

The next owner of the Grange was the attorney and estate agent, Edward Wooley, followed by Josiah Copshut Twistleton, and in 1812 Benjamin Horner. Horner's family sold the Grange to Charles Harris for £9,800, with land comprising 14 acres, 2 rods and 11 poles in area. A succession

Drawing of Fulford Grange, 1894

of other owners followed, until it was on the market once again in 1868. It was described as having a large entrance hall, dining room, morning room, six principal bedrooms, two dressing rooms, two w.c.'s, five servants' bedrooms, and housekeeper's room. The grounds included 'outbuildings, lodge, gardener's cottage, brewhouse, laundry, double coach-house, stabling for six horses, harness room, hay and corn chambers, poultry house and piggeries. There were also tastefully laid-out pleasure gardens, fruitful vineries and greenhouses, with three acres of land and eleven acres of valuable parklike grassland studded with ornamental fruit trees, the whole fourteen acres being in a ring fence'. There was also a riding school and lawn tennis grounds, and the trees included limes, sycamores, poplars, oaks, elms, purple and plain beeches, chestnuts, acacias, yews, and red thorns. The rockery was advertised as being 'largely composed of stones from York Minster and Bradford'. At this time the Pikeing Well (see chapter 14), was part of the estate.

It was the Army contractor Ambrose Walker and his nephew John Phillips Walker who bought the property for £7,200. Eight years later it was sold again, this time to Isaac Poad, the corn and potato merchant. Poad had come to York in 1863 and was the senior partner in the firm of Isaac Poad and Sons, which was based in Walmgate.

On 12th June 1894, Messrs Thomas Walker advertised the auction of the Grange, which included 'the estate of ten acres and then the spacious mansion, formerly the residence of Lady Hartley, in the Italian style of architecture'. But Poad did not in fact sell until October 1899, to William Bentley, for the sum of £2927. By this time the estate had been divided up, and Bentley only bought a part of it. The rest was conveyed by indenture between Poad and Ambrose Walker, William Silversides and Richard Melrose.

Although Walker was the contractor who laid out the new streets on the estate, it was Poad who selected the names. Poad had originated from the North York Moors, and was baptised in Rosedale, so he chose names from that area. They were Rosedale, Farndale, Hartoft, Lastingham and Levisham Streets. The first three streets are named after moors, and the other two after villages. In 1879, entrances were created onto the New Walk, with steps leading down from both Farndale and Hartoft Streets. In 1902, the Gardener's Cottage was occupied by George Pulleyn and a Mr Watherston, who may have been the same man who ran the Brunswick Hotel on Fishergate (see chapter 11).

Gardener's Cottage, Grange Estate, 1996

Poad died on 8th May 1901, aged 66, and eleven years later his wife joined him in the same grave in York cemetery, which is marked by a pink obelisk. He left the parcel of land at the junction of Grange Garth and Fulford Road, to the citizens of York. In 1974, complaints were made about the neglected state of this land. Eight years earlier, in 1966, the press reported that a road which had been closed during the war, which bisected the triangle formed by Grange Street, Grange Garth and Fulford Road, was discovered again by the residents. An application to re-open this 'lost road' was approved.

Alderman William Bentley JP,
Lord Mayor of York

William Bentley, the Lord Mayor who died in office in 1907, organised various charitable events at the Grange in aid of York County Hospital, including a Japanese fete, during his second year as Sheriff. Hundreds of children in national costume, gave a display of the dances of the period and a group of Japanese men and women were in attendance. He also opened the grounds to visitors, and according to his biography 'William Bentley',

"He made other lives beautiful by inviting not only the wealthy, but the poor and the forlorn to spend a quiet afternoon or to meet for social recreation on summer evenings in his beautiful grounds by the Ouse."

After his death, Bentley's wife and son remained in the Grange until 1928 when it was sold to Robert Pulleyn for £3400. Two months later, the Gardener's Cottage was sold to Arthur Sollitt.

In 1932 there were several streets off Grange Garth, bearing the names of Grange Crescent, Grange Grove, Grange Street, and Grange Croft. The latter had several attractively-named houses called The Croft, The Haven, The Poplars and The Nook. Now only Grange Street and Grange Garth remain. In 1939 the Grange was requisitioned by the army. The house is now divided into three quite separate residences - the Grange, the Croft and number 37 Grange Garth.

Grange Street has a range of tall terraced houses. On the corner is Durham House, a hotel, which was once Cambridge Villa. Above the door of number 12, the name of Miss Ripley, music teacher in the 1930s, can still be seen, etched in the glass.

It is rumoured that the comedian Frankie Howerd lived in Hartoft Street for a time, with his aunt, but his autobiography makes no mention of the city. On the corner of Rosedale and Hartoft is an old lamp, with its original on/off switch, which would once have been operated manually. It is a sign of the times that in Hartoft Street, like other terraced streets in the area, there are five visible burglar alarm systems, where once the people who lived there would have always left their doors open.

3

From Nursery to Terrace

By 1854, most of the land on the road to Fulford had become nursery grounds. John Lund's map of Walmgate Stray shows Fulford Road to be 'Ground Not Common', which would have passed through a succession of landlords. Thomas Rigg, the nursery and seedsman, advertised his land in Fishergate as early as 1797. He was assisted in the work by his sons Thomas junior, who ran the Haymarket business, and John, who lived in Fishergate. Theirs was a tragic family history. Thomas outlived three of his four children and fifteen of his grandchildren. John died in 1833 at the age of 57 and his wife Ann continued the nursery business. Only two of their fourteen children survived beyond the age of twenty. Six died in a boating accident in 1830 and are commemorated by a monument in the churchyard of St Lawrence's church. Thomas junior died aged only 37 in 1811, and only two of his five children survived to adulthood. The family shop in Haymarket was closed in 1816 and in 1833 thirty acres was up for sale, followed in 1835 by the market garden. By February 1836 it had been bought by the Backhouses.

James Backhouse occupied three nurseries on Fishergate and part of Cemetery Road. James and his brother Thomas were regarded as one of the greatest firms of botanical nurserymen in England, being pioneers in the cultivation of many rare plants, which James had brought back from his travels in Australasia. They also had nurseries in Acomb, Poppleton Road and Toft Green. Their gardens were described as the 'Northern Kew'. There was also a James Backhouse Cricket team in York at the time.

The land adjoining Backhouse's was the property of George Clarkson, a seedsman, gardener and florist, who had inherited it from J. Brook, who had in turn inherited it from James Fryer, the owner since the mid-18th century. These nurseries lay between the York city boundary and the village of Fulford, in the township of Gate Fulford. Some of the original rocks from the nursery now make up Backhouse's Rockery in York Cemetery.

When Clarkson, who had been a respected nurseryman for many years, died in 1853, he bequeathed the land to his brother, the Reverend William Clarkson, a Wesleyan Minister from Bridlington. William Clarkson decided to sell, and Messrs Acton & Son auctioned the land for him on 24th January 1854, in two separate lots which were described in the Yorkshire Gazette of 14th January, as '14 acres of valuable nursery grounds stocked with forest and fruit trees, roses and shrubs'. Included in the sale were two dwelling-houses, three-storied brick buildings with stone coping on the south gable parapet, fronting Fulford Road (later numbers 196 and 198, part of a row of shops), together with a shop, greenhouse and other smaller outbuildings. The land extended from the main road to the river.

In the absence of a nurseryman coming forward to purchase the two lots in their entirety, the auction resulted in the land being broken up into smaller lots which were sold to individual builders. The first twelve lots (each being 70' 7" wide and 154' 6" long) formed a new street called Alma Terrace, sloping down from Fulford Road to the New Walk.

The first purchaser of land in Alma Terrace was George Simpson, a joiner, builder and one-time clothier of Livingston Street, Leeman Road. Simpson bought lots 6 to 9 in 1855, and built six houses initially, and later a further twelve which were collectively called South View, Alma Terrace. Today these are numbers 40-74 (even numbers) Alma Terrace. On 10th October of the same year, Thomas Thomas, a fruiterer by trade, purchased lots 11 and 12, which backed on to the Grange Estate to the south, and there he built three houses.

In February 1856, John Cattle bought lot 10, and the following month lots 1 to 3 were sold to Joseph Mason, and lots 4 and 5 to Henry Davis. For many of the contracts of sale, Joseph Agar acted as mortgagee, succeeded after his death by his legal representatives Benjamin Agar, Francis Taylor and Robinson Rocliffe. It seems that it was Agar's money which largely built the Terrace.

Fifty yards east of Alma Terrace, a much larger house than those within the terrace was offered for sale in the Gazette of August 1857, (to be auctioned at Hardcastle's Barrack Tavern, the public house opposite),

"All that newly erected and convenient dwelling house with outbuildings and greenhouse adjoining and 2420 square yards of first rate garden ground well stocked with thriving fruit trees, shrubs etc. Sheltered by the Grange Plantation on the north with garden ground in front and on both sides, will be found worthy of attention either as a pleasant suburban cottage or eligible situation for a gardener or florist or as good investment for capital."

By 1861, this was named Briar House, and was occupied by 54 year-old William Cooper, a wine and spirit merchant, his wife Mary, four children and three servants. After the death of his wife in 1862, Cooper commissioned a stained glass memorial to her in the church of St Crux in the Shambles. In 1874, Cooper extended the grounds by buying a plot of land in Alma Terrace from C.J. Peacock for £550, and by February 1913, when the land was drained for its new owner F. Chapman, it included two coach-houses, two greenhouses, stables and pigsties.

In the 1920s it became offices for the Forestry Commission, and then in 1963 a hotel. In 1973 part of the grounds which once supported Victoria plum trees, pear trees near the outer wall, and a weeping willow on the corner, were sold as a residential development site. The following year, a block of eighteen apartments was built there and named Arncliffe Mews. The original plaque for Briar House can still be seen on the wall on Fulford Road.

All the land between the Barrack Tavern and the Cemetery of 1837 formed an estate owned by the Lord Mayor Joseph Agar (descendant of the Agar who acted as Simpson's mortgagee), who lived in Kilburn House, separated from the main road by avenues of trees. The house was built in the early 19th century, and was the home of Amelia Emily Cholmley until her death in 1874, at the age of 90. She was the sister of Colonel Cholmley of Howsham and Whitby Abbey and whilst in York she donated money for a schoolroom at Fulford. After her death an organ costing £600 was installed in Fulford Church in her memory.

By 1876, Agar had bought the house and changed the name from Fulford Lodge to Kilburn House, as his family had originated from Kilburn, in North Yorkshire, home of the White Horse and Thompson, the mouse-man. The gardener lived in the much smaller Kilburn Lodge, and Kilburn Road was also built, facing onto the Low Moor. There are allotments at the bottom of this street today.

Agar was Mayor in 1881-2, 1888-9 and 1889-90, and managed a tannery business, Agar and Chadwick, in Spen Lane. He was a prominent figure in the area, being a steward at Melbourne Terrace Chapel, and Guardian of St Andrew's Parish. Born in 1833, he lived at the House with his wife and three children, eventually dying in July 1920, at the age of 87.

One local man, Mr George Kent, remembers,

We used to call him Daddy Agar, he was an Alderman. He always used to ride in a carriage and pair, and always wore a cloak and a silk hat.

After Agar's death, the house was demolished and the estate split up. Edgeware Road, Kensal Villas, Kensal Rise and Maida Grove were set out, and reputedly given these names because the builders thought that Kilburn House was named after the Kilburn in London! At the top of Kilburn Road were built the Post Office of 1933, and the Christian Science Church of 1928, next door to the Barrack Tavern. It is also interesting to note that a windmill stood on the site in 1736, approximately where Maida Grove is now located, although its exact position is not absolutely clear from John Lund's map. The post office replaced the one which had been at 21 Fishergate in 1900. The building plan, when approved in 1932, consisted of a public office, sub-postmaster's room, clerk's room, instrument room and women's retiring room.

As well as Agar, at least seven other Lord Mayors have come from this area. The earliest mayor to be buried in York Cemetery is William Hutchinson Hearon, tea dealer of Hearon and Dale of High Ousegate, who was Mayor in 1815 and 1827. He owned land near Fishergate Bar where the stone foundations of a church were discovered, along with human skulls and skeletons. This was almost certainly the remains of All Saints' Church, Fishergate. Hearon died on 1st June 1842 at the age of 70 and is remembered by a two foot high chest tomb in the cemetery. In 1880, William Wilkinson Wilberforce, son of the chicory merchant Henry Wilberforce, became Mayor. In 1873 he had lived at Fishergate Villa. He was not directly related to the eminent statesman of the same name, although the latter did visit York for political rallies before his death in 1833. Wilberforce, the Mayor, died in 1895.

William Bentley, who is mentioned in chapter 2, was another Mayor, as was Thomas Morris, a building contractor since 1897 and an active catholic, who lived in Escrick Terrace and was councillor for Walmgate and then Fishergate before being Mayor in 1936-7. His business is still continued today by his grandsons. Edward Lacy, a painter and decorator with a business in Colliergate, lived at 9 New Walk

Terrace, and was Mayor in 1942-3. His grandson became a Methodist minister. Richard Scruton lived at the New Bungalow in Grange Garth, which became 'Littlecroft', and was proprietor of the Ideal Laundry in Trinity Lane. He was York's 488th Lord Mayor, in the year of the city's 1900th anniversary celebrations in 1971. Ten years later Scruton died, having dedicated much of his life to the council and the city, and being made an honorary alderman before his death. His father Walter, a solicitor, had lived at 37 Grange Garth (part of the original Grange building), and his uncle Alfred, Managing Director of Raimes Drug Manufacturers, lived at Watergate, a big house adjoining the Gardener's Cottage at the foot of Grange Garth, and facing the New Walk.

The most recent Lord Mayor from this district is John Boardman, one-time teacher at Fulford School, who lives in Ambrose Street, and was in office from 1995-6.

Hollycroft Estate

About 140 yards from Briar House along the road to Fulford, another substantial property, Holly Croft House, was built on what remained of Clarkson's land. In 1859, this was owned by John Bellerby, the timber merchant, builder and match manufacturer, whose businesses were located at St George's works in Piccadilly and the George Street sawmills. Bellerby died at Holly Croft on 6th November 1874, at the age of 67. Although his son John junior took over the businesses, the estate was sold to Ambrose Walker in 1878. Walker was a prominent army contractor and freeman of the city, who gradually came to own a large amount of property in York.

In 1879, he had laid out Holly Croft Estate into a pattern of streets for building purposes. Just as Clarkson had done with Alma Terrace, Walker contracted separate lots to small builders. One of the first of these was John William Brown Lee, a Lancashire-born builder and bricklayer who lived in Bishophill with his wife and three children. On 29 November

1879, Lee signed a covenant with Ambrose Walker, purchasing 2101 square yards of land, on which he built fifteen terraced houses. These would eventually form numbers 42 to 56 of a new street called Frances Street, incorporating half that street on the south side, bounded to the west by a side road running parallel with the River Ouse.

In the early 1980s, a resident of this street renovated the three outhouses behind his house (coalhouse, lavatory and shed) and found a piece of wood which had supported the old lavatory cistern. When the wood was removed, the word LEE was stamped into the wood in two places. About the same time, another resident removed the layers of paint on his bedroom door with a blow-lamp, and discovered beneath it, a name pencilled on the original wood. It read MOTHER LEE'S COTTAGES. At that time, the name seemed meaningless, but the subsequent discovery that the houses were built by John Lee, led to the supposition that the street was named after John Lee's wife, Fanny (Frances), who tragically died of consumption at the age of 45, on 15 July 1882. There is, however, a second possibility; that the street was named after Ambrose Walker's niece, Francis, (spelt with an I) who was born in 1879. In his will of 1896, Ambrose left a sum of money in trust for her; her father, John Phillips Walker, having been Ambrose's closest relative. There has always been a debate about the spelling of the street name. For many years it was spelled FRANCIS, but later altered to FRANCES, which appears on house deeds, and on the actual street sign, and is now accepted as accurate.

In 1881, John Lee lived at 7 and a half Bishophill, and was the employer of '2.5 men', (probably two men and an adolescent) according to the census. He was then 46 years old, and his wife was three years younger. There is a grave in York cemetery to 'Fanny, beloved wife of J W B Lee, builder of this city'. She was born in 1837 and died 1882. In 1893, John Lee died at the age of 59 and joined his wife there.

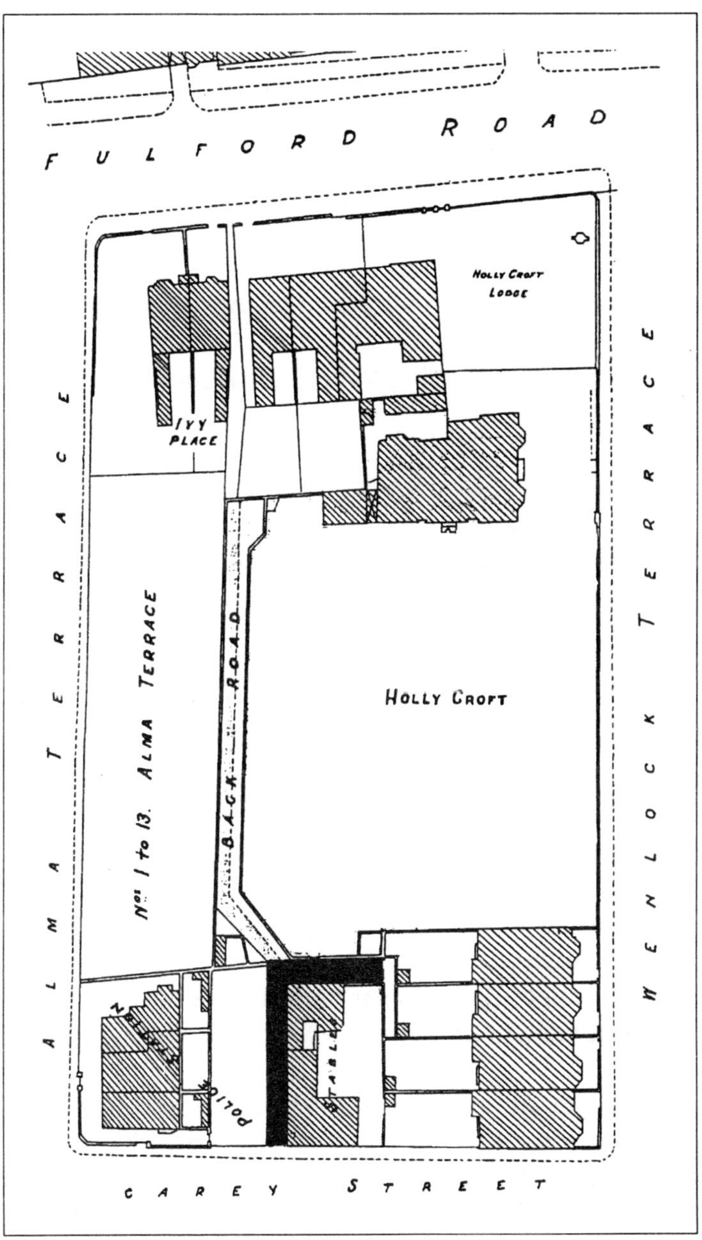

Plan of Hollycroft Estate

Walker continued to sell plots in the street. Joseph Morton, a joiner from Elmwood Street, borrowed the sum of £160 from a local chemist and druggist, Charles Croskell (of 'Croskell's Yellow Mixture', a famous local cure-all), and built several houses on the opposite side to Lee's, adjoining a group of houses built by William Hodge. Thomas Wray, who built numbers 29 to 41 in 1880, had formerly been part of the firm of Wray & Sons, builders, bricklayers and contractors of Darlington. He moved to York and lived there until his retirement and early death in 1902. He had borrowed £2,100 from Walker to enable him to construct the thirteen houses. When, in 1888, J. Elcoat of Smales Street built numbers 81-82 (one building), 84 and 85, all designed by Walter Penty, the street was complete.

Forty yards west of Frances Street, the emergence of another new street in 1881, resulted in three parallel terraces lying on a gentle incline rising from the Ouse to Fulford Road, and connected by Carey Street. There is no definite evidence but Carey Street is likely to have been the work of Henry Carey, a well-known local builder and contractor to the War Department at this period. It was often the practice of 19th-century builders to name streets after their wives or children, but as Ambrose Walker remained unmarried at his death, he named the third terrace after himself, Ambrose Street. Amongst the many bequests of expensive items of jewellery and fine art in his will was a set of marble statues of Chaucer, Dryden, Shakespeare and Milton. The latter two statues were left to Mary Elizabeth Carey, who was perhaps related to Henry Carey! There have been many rumours concerning the origin of the street names, including the idea that the streets were named after the daughters of Lord Wenlock, but as their names were not Alma, Frances or Ambrose, this is obviously unfounded.

The original plan and layout of Ambrose Street, surveyed by W G Penty, divided the street, naming the two sides Ambrose Street North and Ambrose Street South. Half of the street on the south side was contracted to Edward Keswick, one of three builder brothers, in June 1881. His brothers, John and Charles, built eight houses between them. However, the trio defaulted on payments to the mortgagees, the Ebor Permanent Building Society, to the value of £1800, and the land thus reverted to the society. George Jennings and Edwin Potter had bought the land to the east and west respectively, and Robert Penty, a joiner and cabinet maker from Heslington, built a further batch of houses in the street.

The building of these streets coincided with the national late 19th-century building boom which collapsed in about 1901 due to the over-production of houses. The group of streets, though obviously working class, housed mostly skilled workers. In 1885, a sample of their occupations included whitesmith, glass blower, clockmaker, bookbinder, weaver, bottle stopper, matchmaker, sewing machine agent, railway inspector, pattern maker, cattle dealer and coachman, as well as quite a number of tram drivers from the depot at Fulford Cross. Probably one of the most interesting was William Addy, the lamplighter, who lived at 101 Alma Terrace from the 1890s (thirty years after Fulford was first lit with gas in 1862) until the First World War. He was certainly a notable feature of the neighbourhood as George Kent was aware,

The lamplighter used to live in the bottom house, called him Addy. He used to come round, it was all gas lamps in those days, push a pole up to light it as soon as ever it started to get dark, then in the morning put it out. It had a hook on it and when there was an air-raid warning, he used to race up the streets, the lights used to go down and then up again and down and out. That was to give us the warning.

Many professions were connected with the Barracks. Apart from soldiers of various ranks, there was an army shoemaker, an army scripture reader and several army musicians. One of these, Frank Liddle, who lived at 13 Alma Terrace in 1881, reputedly composed several well-known hymn tunes.

During 1882-3, a further street appeared, branching out of Carey Street, towards Fulford Road. Wenlock Terrace, as it was called, was rather different in that it provided accommodation for the professional classes. The five-storied houses, including basement (servants' quarters) and attic, are the tallest Victorian houses in the city, and are splendidly Gothic in character. Their steep pitched roofs and decorative towers, added to the ornamental ridge tiles at the apex of the roof, resemble some types of mediaeval architecture. Many of the houses display corbels depicting cherubs, dragons, and fierce gargoyles, resting on pillars of fleurs-de-lys. One side (numbers 14 to 17), next to the grounds of Holly Croft, was built by John and Thomas Biscomb, who were responsible for houses in Hartoft Street on the Grange estate. The first occupants of the new terrace included the Chaplain to the Forces, an army major, Miss Wilson's Ladies' College, the general postmaster, an official receiver in bankruptcy, a captain in the 3rd Hussars, the manager of the Tadcaster Tower Brewery Company, who was also a councillor (Howard Tripp), and the acclaimed York architect, Walter Penty. Several houses still belonged to Ambrose Walker who commanded rents of at least £50 p.a. for them, in contrast to Lee's houses in Frances Street which only brought in £9 10s a year.

In 1903, Holly Croft was sold by Major Harold Sykes, of the 2nd Dragoon Guards or Scots Greys (who had bought it for £2,000 from Walker's estate in April 1899) to the Secretary of State for the War Department. The house was later used as the Headquarters of PAYE Command, and MOD offices during World War II.

According to Walker's layout of the streets, Wenlock Terrace was at first named Holly Terrace, because it incorporated Holly Croft. The name was changed fairly rapidly. The 3rd Baron Wenlock of Escrick, Beilby Lawley, was a popular landowner of the period who had strong ties with the army. Several streets in York and Escrick were named after Lord Wenlock after he was made a freeman of the city, though he had no direct connection with the layout and building.

Hollycroft, 1996

The final portion of land to complete the block of streets faced the river at the foot of the three parallel terraces, and this was sold to Francis Rawling by Walker in August 1880. It eventually became Holly Terrace, though the houses were at first numbered as part of New Walk. They were built in two stages. The first eight, between Ambrose Street and Frances Street, were three-storied, slightly resembling Wenlock Terrace in their mock Gothic detail, though much less ornate. Some time later (by 1898) another four houses were added, between Alma Terrace and Frances Street, rather smaller in size. The numbering led to a great deal of confusion because it did not follow in sequence and it was not until 1967 that the confusion was finally rectified.

In 1901, two gas lamps were removed from Holly Terrace by the council to light New Walk. Obviously the need to light the riverside must have been greater!

Unfortunately Holly Terrace, and Lastingham Terrace, the houses which face the river at the foot of Hartoft Street and Farndale Street, further along, do not feature on any York street maps. Visitors to the streets find great difficulty in locating them, which is particularly worrying for those expecting workmen and ambulances.

Ambrose Walker died in August 1896 at the age of 76. At the end of his life, his occupation was given as 'gentleman' rather than the contractor of earlier years. He actually started out in the building trade, and was a planemaker when he became a Freeman of the City in 1843. Unlike his brother John, he did not follow in the footsteps of his father Peter Walker, whose trade was that of a butcher. Ambrose certainly moved around the area during his lifetime, from Fishergate House in 1868 to Melbourne Terrace, and then New Walk Terrace in 1872, to the Grange 1874, and to Holly Croft in 1879. Having done as much as he could to develop these estates, he moved to Chelmsford House in 1881, and a few months later to the Manor House, also on Chelmsford Place. By 1885 he was at number 7 Chelmsford Place. Ambrose had made a considerable fortune from his career and was a man of elegant appearance and tastes. He always wore a scarf pin, and often a double-headed snake ring with two diamond eyes, and another ring in the shape of a dog's head set with seven diamonds. He is buried in the old Fulford churchyard at the bottom of St Oswald's Road and his stone reads 'Thy statutes have been my song in the house of my pilgrimage'.

4

The Military Connection

Military Sunday was inaugurated in April 1885 by the Very Rev the Dean, A P Purey Cust, in memory of General Gordon, who was killed at Khartoum that year. The first parade saw troops from the West Yorkshire Regiment, the 3rd King's Own Hussars, and the Commissariat Unit, together with details from the Ordnance and 1st East Riding Volunteers, who marched from both Barracks through the city to the Minster, where a commemorative service was held. The occasion proved so immensely popular with the citizens of York that it was made an annual event up until 1939. Farm labourers and their families would come into the city in droves from the countryside. One of the attractions was that the troops all wore full-dress uniform, and presented a most colourful and spectacular scene, in scarlet and blue with gold and silver trappings, complete with plumed hats and busbies.

Most of the residents of Fulford would turn out in their Sunday best and stand at intervals along Fulford Road, to get a good view of the passing parade, with its soldiers on horseback and marching infantry bands. One of the best-loved regiments was the Scots Greys who went out to France in 1914 and, as one man explained, 'they was cut to ribbons...we never saw 'em anymore'. They were certainly stunning in red tunics, blue trousers with yellow braid and large busbies. The military funeral in this photograph took place in about 1913. It might have been that of Corporal Dubock who drowned at the end of New Walk whilst saving the life of a young child. Only a week before, he had fought Wally Chipper (son of the traffic manager of the City of York Tramways of 3 Alma Terrace) at the boxing ring in Fishergate. Dubock was taken to the mortuary at the

Military Hospital on Fulford Road. At his funeral, the regiment lined the road to the cemetery and one horse was led with boots 'reverse order'.

Military Funeral, 1913

The Yorkshire Gazette of April 1879 reported the death in Fulford of 67 year old James Bolton, of the 4th Light Dragoons. Bolton had taken part in the celebrated charge of the Light Brigade at the Battle of Balaclava in October 1854, which resulted in huge British casualties. Interestingly, his funeral service was performed by Eustace Tennyson D'Eyncourt Jesse, father of the novelist F Tennyson Jesse, and curate of Fulford from 1878 until 1881, when he moved to London. It is quite a co-incidence that this cleric was the nephew of Alfred Lord Tennyson, author of the famous poem 'The Charge of the Light Brigade' and happened to be in York at the time of Bolton's death. Tennyson also went on to write another poem about the battle, 'Charge of the Heavy Brigade at Balaclava' but this did not receive the acclaim of the first epic.

By 1880, Fulford had been the home of the army barracks for many years. The Cavalry Barracks, designed by James Johnson and John Sanders, and built by William Pitt, were erected in 1792, at a cost of £25,000 for twelve acres of ground, with accommodation for three field officers, five captains, nine subalterns and staff, four quartermasters, 240 NCOs and privates, and 266 horses. It was considerably enlarged (to thirty acres) and improved in 1861. Outside the barracks were two crossed lancers, and this was the home for many years of the 16th and 19th Lancers. The Royal Arms were modelled in Coade stone and dated 1796.

18th Hussars changing the guard at Cavalry Barracks

Andy Waudby remembers visiting the barracks as a child, and seeing,

A squad of soldiers with blue serge uniforms and on their tunics they have lovely golden braid going around the front. They wear black riding boots and spurs, and they have a round hat with a white plume. And these are the Yorkshire Hussars.

In their hands they have long swords called sabres, they are doing sabre drill. At the side of the road there are a column of horses coming up the road and turning into the Barracks. These soldiers have khaki uniforms with brass buttons, khaki riding breeches, with puttees wrapped round their legs just below the knees, and shiny spurs on their boots. And each wears a peaked cap with a badge. In their right hand each soldier holds a lance with a white and red flag. The harness on the horses was that polished, they glinted in the sunlight.

Entrance to Cavalry Barracks

The Barracks were open to the public on Sundays, and soon became the scene of regular family outings. Adults and children alike flocked to watch the horses being groomed; the soldiers were said to be so conscientious that they would feed, water and groom each horse before consuming their own breakfasts. Children would also find the place very attractive, not least because their services were frequently needed just before a big parade such as Empire Day or Military Sunday. They could earn sixpence to clean and pipe-clay the badges and mail-chain epaulettes. Cleaning the whole harness and polishing all the leather might mean a whole shilling. Additionally, some were given 'hard tack', the tins of iron ration which proved to be too hard to eat.

In 1874 there was a military circus held there for a week. Performances included circus acts and re-enactments of battles of the Ashanti and other wars, and took place in the riding-school at the rear, on Low Moor where riders practised their jumps.

Between 1877 and 1880 the Infantry (now Imphal) Barracks were built further down the road on the edge of Fulford Village, at a cost of £150,000. The castle keep at the entrance is known to local children as the marmalade jar.

Infantry Barracks

Mr Ray Close visited the barracks as a child,

On the square in the infantry barracks they used to have four First World tanks stood at each corner of the square. When the war came along, they were all melted down for scrap metal.

These establishments were to have a profound impact on the life of the residents in the district. Names with military associations had begun to spring up in the city, and it is almost certain that Alma Terrace was named after the Battle of the Alma, Alma-ata, Southern Russia. This decisive battle took place at the beginning of the Crimean War in 1854, a year before the terrace was built.

There was an even closer connection with the Barracks. Between 1869 and 1892, a large number of girls from the area were married at Saint Oswald's Church, Fulford, and over two-thirds of these weddings were to soldiers from the Barracks. There would also inevitably be many liaisons which did not end in marriage.

Millie Fenn recalls,

Frances Street was out of bounds to soldiers, because of a woman at the bottom of the street. She ran through the passage as drunk as a skuttle, and a soldier came out later. They were shouting and bawling.

Yet the soldiers were a source of income for local children. Helen Wildon, whose family lived at Phoenix Cottage on Castle Mills Bridge in 1907, regularly ran errands for the soldiers, though her strict elder sister was kept ignorant of this,

I used to take fish and chips to the barracks. The lads used to come and say, 'Can you send thirty wrappings of fish and chips?' It was a penny for one of each and you could get h'apporth of chips. I had to take a basket and they'd paid for them

before I got them and they used to give me threepence to go. Friday night I had to call in the Band of Hope. I took my fish and chips in with me, to get my card stamped to say I'd been. My sister didn't know about the fish and chips. We had to give our names down to recite or sing. I'd put my name down the Friday before and I'd forgotten. I'd just been listening to the tingalarie outside, and I started to sing (a common song that was all the go then) and I sang, taking off the music halls, and the chief said, 'That'll do, Ellen, that'll do nicely. We don't sing that kind of song in the Band of Hope'. I'd only be about ten years old. We sang 'Water is Best', 'Give said the little stream, give oh give'. When I went to work at Rowntrees, he was our head man, and he remembered about that.

Walter Atkin was a paper boy in Fishergate in 1914. He delivered to the Barracks,

The shop I worked for was in Fishergate (Gilbertsons) and we had to be there at 6.30 am because people expected their papers to read at the breakfast table. Sometimes Mr G asked a couple of the lads to work all day Saturday, paying us a little extra, but also paid commission on most of the stuff we sold. This job meant packing your bag with periodicals, paperback books, writing paper, envelopes and little bottles of ink complete with a wood pen with a steel nib. These articles we could take to the Barracks on Fulford Road, one to the Cavalry Barracks, the other to the Infantry Barracks. The guards let us through the gates and we would then visit the rooms to sell our goods.

I liked the Cavalry best, long two-storied blocks around a square, the ground floor was made up of stables with harness rooms. I loved to watch the squaddies grooming and brushing the horses until their coats shone. The upper floor was the living and sleeping quarters, long rooms with rows of beds and men off duty either reading, playing cards or writing home and maybe the odd long horn gramophone would be playing. Generally all the chaps were good to us, would buy our goods, sometimes adding the extra copper, which on their pay I should imagine was really OK.

I learned to be a good salesman, sometimes I would be asked if I had any sisters. I had two and told them so, but not until I'd finished a room did I say, if mother would let me I'd bring the girls to see them, even in the pram, because both were much younger than me. This usually got a roar of laughter on the chap who'd asked.

Whoever finished his barracks first would then go across the road to the Military Hospital, leaving word with the sentry for one's mate. The hospital staff would allow us to enter some of the wards to sell our stuff, other wards a nurse or orderly would keep us at the door and shout down the ward asking who wanted what. We always felt we had done a good job, both for the soldiers and our boss, not forgetting any commission earned by us. Happy but hard and tiring jobs, and really thankful for the shilling or two we took home to Ma.

Winners of Regimental Pushball Competition
Cavalry Barracks, 1905

Ken Richmond worked at the Barracks in the 1970s,

I used to do rations for all the messes, the Headquarters and Officers' Mess, Sergeants' Mess and other ranks. Used to collect 'em from Strensall three times a week and then up to Catterick for the compo rations and all the heavy gear used in exercises. I think it's all computerised now, but we used to have to write it all out in longhand every day. There were all sorts, the different range of foods was terrific really.

I allus remember when the Queen came to open the new Officers' Mess, and the food that was put on. She brought her own chefs with her and I suppose they'd do the main meals, but the cooks did little tiny fancy cakes. And I remember I had to get some Earl Grey tea, the sort the Queen likes. They used to order all these fancy things, caviar and quails' eggs. The Mess was up a slope and the car she came in had to go up and they was afraid the undercarriage would catch as it mounted the pavement to go into the Mess. They had it all altered, it was a right rush.

In 1977 after the Cavalry Barracks had lain empty for some years, work began on the buildings to create the new City Police Headquarters, which had previously been based in Clifford Street. Some buildings were renovated, others demolished. The place was fully operational by August 1979. Ken Richmond recalls,

When they eventually pulled them [the stables] down, they found all sorts of games and things what soldiers had played maybe a hundred years before, cards and a lot of different games and dice.

The Garrison church of St George's was built for the barracks, and the 18th Hussars and other regiments could be seen marching to church each Sunday. Today the building is only used as a store for lost property for the police station, and is full of all sorts of missing equipment. As well as the more conventional items, there are bicycles, typewriters and even a

18th Hussars Church Parade

boat waiting to be reclaimed. The cobbles in the layby outside, and the horse trough have gone, and a bench and two telephone kiosks stand in front of the original entrance to the Cavalry Barracks, which is now bricked up. Between the police station and the Barrack Tavern, there is now a new building (from the 1990s) called Frederick House. This is part of Shepherd's Building Group.

Many of the houses in Fishergate and Fulford Road were used at some time for military purposes. On the corner of Melbourne Terrace, was the War Office, or headquarters of Northern Command. It was built in 1878 in mock-Tudor style, and designed by the War Department's own architects, when the Headquarters was transferred from Manchester to York. It was the same year that the trams began running to the Fulford depot. On the tower is a weather vane with a symbol in the shape of the suit of clubs in a pack of cards. The War Office, even in peacetime, was a

Parade at St George's Garrison Church, Cavalry Barracks

War Office

place full of clerical soldiers, civil servants, and messengers in uniform, who were mostly ex-servicemen.

Today the office is called Tower House, and is a business conference centre. After being decommissioned by the Ministry of Defence, it was let in small units for ten years. The inside was completely gutted and rebuilt as offices. In the late 1970s approval was sought for a geriatric centre, then a hotel, and even the consulting rooms of a hypnotist. It was withdrawn from public auction in 1980 when it failed to reach the reserve price of £65,000 and was sold to a consortium of York buyers. A few years ago when the roof was being repaired, the builders found a way to make the clock strike thirteen on several occasions throughout the day, much to the consternation of local residents, some of whom regarded this as most unlucky.

The Soldiers' Home

In 1909 one of the houses in Wenlock Terrace, number 16, was bought by a Scottish woman who had already been given the title 'Florence Nightingale of the 20th century'. Mabel Caroline Carmichael Walker had left her home in Dumfriesshire in 1897 to take her delicate sister abroad for her health. Whilst they were in Pietermaritzburg, Natal, the South African War broke out. Miss Walker felt that the British soldiers fighting out there ought to have a place where they could relax and unwind and feel 'a sense of England', although they were so far from home. She opened her own house to those stationed in the district, and provided musical evenings, games, tea and sandwiches. She spent much of her private fortune during the eleven year stay in that country, organising canteens for the soldiers.

When she returned to Britain, General Menzies, one of her relatives stationed in York, urged her to open a similar Soldiers' Home in the city. Another lady, Miss Erskine, ran a home for the troops in a little house near to the barracks, which had been opened in 1908 by Brigadier

General Altham. The house had failed and so was sold, with the proceeds being handed over to the Soldiers' Institute in Strensall Camp. Miss Carmichael-Walker opened her Home in Wenlock Terrace, later purchasing the two adjoining houses and having communicating passages tunnelled between them. One such passage was so high and narrow that it was nicknamed 'The Trench'. The home comprised a drawing-room used for recreation, a dining-room used as a coffee bar,

Soldiers' Home, 1900s

a prayer room where meetings were conducted by an Army Scripture Reader, and bedrooms on the first floor which were occupied by men with weekend passes or travelling through the city. She supplied food, games, billiards, reading and writing rooms and dormitories, and was aided in her work by her invalid sister and several members of staff. Soon she was able to buy the fourth house in the block for the sisters' own use, and when an interested party, Lord Danesford, died, he left her the house opposite for use as married quarters. This became known as the Lord Danesford Memorial Home. The upkeep of the buildings was financed by a group of private voluntary subscribers, together with a small grant from the Army itself. The Patron was HRH Princess Victoria.

In 1912, thirteen different regiments used the Home as well as relations of men who were ill in the nearby Military Hospital. Soon a weekly mother's meeting was started, in addition to the one conducted in the barracks. That year, as well as subscriptions received (of £247), there were also gifts of books, magazines, newspapers, pictures, flowers, bagatelle board, table football and a chest of tea. The Home also held occasional jumble sales and sales of work, to raise funds. Men who had stayed there sent letters from abroad telling how the home had been a support to them. One man wrote, "The home has been the means of keeping me straight. I have always found it to be a Home to those away from home."

Miss Walker soon established herself in the area, and was considered a rather eccentric and delightful person, who travelled everywhere in a donkey and trap. The donkey, whose name was Sally, was stabled in the back lane between the police house and Wenlock Terrace, which was referred to as 'Donkey Lane'. In the garden of number 16 there was a tablet in the wall, above a cairn covered with rockplants, as a memorial to the fallen of the First World War. The inscription read,

"This tablet and cairn are erected by the Misses Carmichael-Walker in memory of many gallant men who made the Soldiers' Institute their home away from home and who gave their lives, at the call of duty in the Great War. Only by the Cross into Life."

Cairn in garden of Soldiers' Home

For many years the cairn and tablet had disappeared but later turned up in Strensall Church. There was also a plaque outside the house, and this was removed and placed in the church adjoining the police station.

In May 1929, Major-General Cameron, Commanding Officer of the 49th (West Riding) Division, officially opened the extensions of the Home. The houses adjoining became a rest room, bedrooms for relatives of men who were seriously ill, accommodation for men on leave, and four sets of quarters for soldiers' families not housed in the Barracks. The chief purposes of the home had always been 'to advance the cause of religion and temperance in the garrison', to provide a social centre for the men, and a 'home away from home'. Its influence was felt throughout

Northern Command. After the official opening ceremony, the Lord Mayor appealed for funds and many donations were received.

By 1930 there were nightly meetings in the Quiet Room for Bible study and prayer. Every Sunday there was a hearty service with hymn singing in the concert room. In September was a big Michaelmas Fair in the Assembly Rooms, with the object of starting funds for another branch near Strensall camp. There were various stalls, a display of classical dancing, the band of the First Battalion Northumberland Fusiliers, and 'talented impersonations of Dickens characters', which made over £65.

During the Second World War, Miss Walker (who had been awarded the CBE) became an official visitor to the wounded in France, so responsibility for the Home was taken over by Miss Ellen Carmichael-Walker, the sister who had been crippled in a street accident. During air-raids the cellars were opened to anyone who needed shelter, and coffee and biscuits were always on hand. In April 1946 the sisters retired to live in Melbourne Terrace and on 10th September 1948 Mabel Carmichael Walker died at the age of 83. She is still warmly remembered not only by the military, but by civilians in the area, who believe that she rendered an invaluable service to others all her life.

The Tattoo

In 1955 the Northern Command decided to hold a Tattoo on the Knavesmire. There had been three tattoos previously in York, in 1929, 1932 and 1933. But 1955 marked the bi-centenary of the King's Own Yorkshire Light Infantry, and it turned out to be a huge event. There were eleven performances (compared with six at the previous year's tattoo in Leeds) and seating was provided for 18,000 with standing room for a further 1,000. Twenty regiments and ten bands took part, including the Royal Corps of Signals army motor cycle team, and the Arab Legion band in their stunning white uniforms and red Shmagh head-dresses. Parachutists were dropped 'into the fray' by balloon behind the backcloth which displayed a reproduction of Micklegate Bar. Soldiers from the RAOC performed, and the Household Cavalry presented a musical ride.

A Bailey Bridge was built by the Royal Engineers from the end of New Walk across to Clementhorpe near the Knavesmire, a foot bridge for army personnel only, so that civilians had to cross the river by other means. Needless to say, the ferry did a roaring trade during the period of the Tattoo, 22nd July to 1st August. The troops would return at about midnight each night, marching over the footbridge in formation, and hundreds would turn out to watch the spectacle. Winnie Richmond vividly remembers the scene,

The brass bands used to play as they came. I think the most marvellous sight was the full Band of the Black Watch, said they were going to play all the way down Ambrose Street and I stood at the bottom and shivered. They took the full width of Ambrose Street up and they were playing and their kilts swinging.

5

The First Police Station

In December 1879 Ambrose Walker sold, to the East Riding Justices, a plot of land measuring 1036 square yards, on the corner of Carey Street and Alma Terrace, which became the site of the Fulford Police Station. Since the 1860s, the terrace had accommodated a police sergeant from the East Riding Constabulary, initially in a private house. In its embryonic days it seems that the station was not kept terribly busy. One of its certain uses, however, must have been to combat the wave of drunkenness which was frequently bemoaned in the local newspapers as a cause of great concern to the police. The three cells in the station are likely to have regularly witnessed the appearance of customers from the Beerhouse further down the terrace.

In the summer of 1897 fourteen more houses were built in Alma Terrace, stretching from Fulford Road to Carey Street, and being numbered 1 to 14, the police station thus becoming number 15/16. The builder was George Moss who also built a block of five houses and four cottages at the river end of the terrace in 1898. The whole terrace had to be re-numbered, and the Beerhouse (once number 28) became number 47. Moss, who was elected as councillor to the Walmgate Ward in 1900, lived in Holly Terrace and was a neighbour of John Henry Rougier, the owner of a comb factory in Rougier Street. When his firm closed down in 1931, it marked the end of this kind of business in England.

In October 1884 the city boundaries were altered, and the district was gathered into the Walmgate ward of York. Being no longer under the jurisdiction of the East Riding, the Police Station was sold to the York

City Corporation in May 1885. After some wrangling about the price, the Town Clerk authorised payment of £1,000 for the station which comprised a charge room, three cells, two dwelling-houses and an area of 826 square yards including a piece of vacant land at the rear. The Chief Constable's report of December 1884 suggested that the station be taken over so that prisoners from the district could be "detained until sober or otherwise and brought to the central station each morning at 6 o'clock". He went on to explain,

"Fulford being an important district on account of its proximity to the barracks and the numerous prostitutes residing in the neighbourhood, I suggest that one inspector reside at Alma Terrace and take charge of the police station, with six night and two day men."

But, according to Frances Finnegan's study of Victorian prostitutes, such a measure did not succeed, because the Penitentiary Society Ladies' Committee reported that inmates of their Refuge were still "catering to the needs of the barracks. They noted in 1887, for example, that Ann Elizabeth Medd, a seventeen year old prostitute from Malton, admitted to the Ladies that she had just spent one month in a brothel in Ambrose Street." Another factor may have been the policemen themselves. Finnegan claims that "one in every six identified clients in 1880 was a policeman".

The Yorkshire Evening Press of 10th January 1885 reported the alleged assault by two foot soldiers from the Barracks, of Anne Greame who kept a 'house of ill-repute' in Frances Street. She accused them of beating her but they denied the charge, claiming that they were 'having a singsong in the room when she rushed upon them with a poker'. The Bench pronounced that all the parties were equally reprehensible and ordered that the sixteen shillings costs be split between them.

The first policeman to be officially appointed in this police station by the York authorities was PC Riley, who was to reside on the premises with his wife who would act as 'female searcher' and agreed to keep the cells and station house clean, for a rent of 2s 6d a week. The Chief Constable was authorised to procure one table, one desk, one stool, one pail, one chair and six rugs for the Station's use. In August this was extended to include a writing-desk and then in December 1885 the station was equipped with fire-fighting apparatus. At the rear of the station was kept a handcart, hose and handpump, together with a shed for the fire engine. In January 1886 it was agreed that the station be connected to the central Police Station by telephone, rather a sophisticated arrangement for the period. It would almost certainly have been the first telephone in the area.

In 1887 the exterior was painted and four years later, in 1891, a new fence wall was erected by one of the Keswick brothers, John, with an iron palisade, reel-house and washhouse. The privies and ashpits were removed in favour of new wc's (quite a luxury at that time) at a cost of £200. The following January a hose-cart and telescopic ladder carriage were purchased from Birmingham Corporation for £20, and when in 1894 a coloured lamp was provided for the front of the station, the renovations were complete. There were both cowsheds and horse stables in the lane behind the police station.

In August 1969 the police station was sold. It had not actually been operating as such for many years. After the First World War it divided into two parts, one a police house and the other a Boys' Remand Home, run by Mr Bates. The Remand Home had been one of several in the city, used to detain boys temporarily as Ken Richmond explains,

Before they altered the front of the house, the front facing Carey Street, there used to be a barred window, like a proper little cell. If you were bad your dad said, 'Put him in t'cell for the night'. Local bobby used to shove you in and all t'kids used to come and poke fun at you. I've never been in myself like, though I used to be a bad lad!

The 'local bobby' was remembered with affection, because 'instead of arresting you, he'd give you a clout with his cape'. From June 1933 until February 1943, PC Fred Mirfield occupied the house. He was well-liked in the area, being a member of York City Rugby Team, the Dreadnoughts (as many policemen were), and renowned for his specially-made heavy-duty green Raleigh bicycle with its double frame and motor cycle seat. He was pensioned in 1942 and died in January 1969. The last policeman to reside in the house was Inspector Duck who left in 1966. At the rear of the station Mr John Taylor, a builder from Alma Terrace, owned 125 square yards of land, and Joseph Smith, the coal merchant, rented a shed and part of the yard, which had previously been the station mortuary used to lay out bodies dragged from the Ouse. After having lain vacant for some time and been subject to vandalism and the theft of lead pipes and copper cylinders, the station was converted, in 1973, to six flats. In March 1978 it became a small hotel, aptly named Copper's Lodge.

Copper's Lodge, 1996

6

The Trams

In 1880 the first horse trams began to operate in York. Lines were laid from Fulford to Nessgate (the new tram depot was located opposite the Infantry Barracks), and later extended up to the Mount. The comprehensive history of this service has been covered elsewhere; but no history of this part of York could appear without mentioning the trams.

The Gazette of 30th October 1880 described the previous day's opening, where Major-General Hutchinson, Inspector to the Board of Trade, made the journey from Castle Mills Bridge to Fulford with two horses 'driven at a satisfactory speed'. He was accompanied by the Lord Mayor, Town Clerk, and City Surveyor, and they made the return journey in a car propelled by steam power. The official trial run took place on 4th December 1880 when the steam tramcar was authorised to run from Fulford to Castle Mills and back several times. The depot at Fulford Cross also included stables and three sidings for repairing carriages. Employees would work on the trams into the night, making sure they were in good condition for the next day. Administrative offices were built after the company (York Tramways Co Ltd) obtained freehold. Fulford Cross had once been the city boundary, and was also known as the 'butter stone' because rural farmworkers journeyed there to sell eggs and butter. Young children grew up with the belief that the octagonal stone was actually filled with butter, and courting couples used the cross as their regular meeting place. Originally country people left food there but would not venture further into the city because of the threat of the plague.

Fulford Cross Tram Depot

Many of the drivers and conductors of the trams resided in the area off Fulford Road. Hugh Murray states in his study of the horse trams of York,

"There was a considerable concentration in three streets - Elmwood Street, Frances Street and Ambrose Street on the west side of Fulford Road. These latter two streets, forming with Alma Terrace, Wenlock Terrace and Carey Street a self-contained complex, were conveniently close to the tramway depot at Fulford Cross."

John Boynton, a tram driver who lived in six different houses in Ambrose Street and Frances Street between 1889 and 1902, was one of only four men who served for more than ten years continuously. Walter Copley was employed for eleven years, but not continuously, and he too lived in six different houses in the area between 1891 and 1909. His tram service was interrupted by his brief spell as a groom in 1900.

In February 1909 the tramway's revised list of stopping places now included Alma Terrace and Wenlock Terrace amongst their number, which continued until the horse trams ceased to run in September 1909. On 10th January 1910, the first York electric tram ran from the depot. Mr George Kent's father drove the passenger cars and he has a card edged in black which reads:

In loving remembrance of the York horse trams
Which ceased to exist at 11.05 pm.
Tuesday September 7th 1909.
Gone but not forgotten.
May they rest in pieces.

He remembers that the fare from,

Alma Terrace to Nessgate was a penny. A tram driver's wage was sixpence an hour and a halfpence extra for being an instructor.

Some residents were not so pleased with the trams. Mr Frederick Atkinson who lived in Alma Terrace remembers,

I got knocked down with a tram car when I first started school. I have a mark there, a girl threw me hat onto t'road and of course I'd just started and I was young and ran onto t'road into t'tram car.

Then there was a policeman called Polly Perkins that lived in Alma Terrace, and he just picked me up and got in t'tram and never bothered to know whether your legs were broken, he just picked you up and took you away. He knew who I was, like, and he knew me father was at home. Polly Perkins gathered me up, they dropped foot board and it trapped me and he put me into t'tram and took me to

Military Hospital and I was stitched up there. I got mark of an old tram, York tram back in 1918.

But it did not stop him travelling by tram,

Well they rattled a bit and that but they got you there you know, you could go and sit on t'top or down below and it was quite cheap, we're talking of pence. He could get to one end and drive it and he would walk to other end and he could take it other way, it was all electrical. And there was overhead wires and when they got to the destination they used to pull thing round and connect it to t'top with cable like a big wheel.

Claire Graham remembers,

The trams used to come down to Fulford and on hot days the water cart used to come with it, like a purple dragon and it had horses all the way round, and you know, it used to cool the line, well that was really an event.

As a child, Andy Waudby found the trams a 'lovely experience', on what were usually nicknamed 'rattlers'. He liked to travel on the top deck, where there were two rows of wooden seats,

In the centre of the tram was a metal pillar, on the top of the pillar was a long metal pole with a wheel on the end which enabled this metal pole to collect the electric off the cables which went along the road. I remember that outside Clark's tobacco shop in Bridge Street was a life-sized figure of Napoleon in his French uniform. Soldiers used to get drunk and when they were going back to the barracks at night, they used to steal Napoleon and take him on top of the tram back to the barracks.

Next morning found Napoleon on guard at the gate of the barracks. Sometimes the soldiers would throw him off Ouse Bridge and send him down the river for a swim. The lock keepers used to find him and take him back to the shop. One could say that Napoleon had done a few guard duties at the barracks.

The last tram ran from Fulford depot on 16th November 1935. The tram sheds were closed down in 1963, the depot having been variously used as an ARP store, REME workshops and finally a garage. The final stage in the history of trams took place in February 1995 when the old depot, lastly Polar Motors, until their removal to Monk's Cross in 1992, was demolished. Children from the Steiner School in Fulford Cross rescued part of the old track, to use in their local history studies. The site is now occupied by Aldi and Iceland supermarkets.

7

The Glassworks

Unlike many other parts of the city, Fishergate was not a hive of industry in the 19th century. In the 1840s a saw mill and lead works were situated there. The saw mill was opposite the grounds of Fishergate House.

After the military connection, the biggest employer in the area was the glassworks. The first works was established in about 1794 by Hampston and Prince, to manufacture flint glass and medicinal phials, and was built on the land of St Andrew's Priory. In 1835 another works was built in York, the York Flint Glass Company, which by 1851 was the largest employer in the city, even bigger than the confectionery firms of Terrys and Cravens. Many glass employees joined the Flint Glassmaker's Friendly Society, whose membership reached 84 in 1877, as it also served as a union.

The process of manufacturing involved a mixture of Lynn sand, pearl ashes and red lead, heated until it formed a molten liquid. The glassworks furnaces were kept burning continuously and the temperature had to be exactly right if the glass were to be shaped properly. Then the glass would be blown, before cooling very slowly. The art of blowing glass by mouth (or colloquially, 'putting your pontil in the gloryhole') is over 2000 years old, and was first performed by the Romans. But in the 19th century, compressed air blowing machines were introduced. Today the process is almost fully automated, though individual glass-blowers do still exist, and the art is not yet dead. Individually blown pieces are now highly collectable.

The process of glass bottle making was done by gangs of five men, each of whom played their own part in the craft. The 'bottle-maker' was in charge of the gang. The 'gatherer' began the work, by placing the molten liquid, called the metal, into the blow-pipe. This was then passed to the 'blower', who would manipulate and blow the bottle into shape. This went to the 'wetter-off' who broke off any superfluous glass from the neck and passed the product to the 'bottle-maker'. His task was to run metal round the neck and fashion it into final shape. The last of the gang, the 'taker-in', was usually a young boy, who would take the bottle over to the annealing kiln where it would cool for 48 hours. The 1881 census for Fishergate includes such occupations as glass stopper, glass cutter, glass stainer and glass blower, which would have encompassed the other more specific roles.

York Glass Company, as it was known, continued trading well into the 19th century eventually becoming Redfearn's National Glass Company in 1930, making glass bottles, jam jars, jars for beauty creams and vinegar bottles amongst other products. The tall imposing tower was an aerial landmark which pinpointed the whole area on any photograph.

Whitakers tanker firm brought crude fuel oil each week up the river from Hull to the wharf at Redfearns, to heat the furnaces. The oil, which resembled thick treacle, was pumped by pipes directly into the back of the works. This was obviously more economical than transporting it by road. A barge would hold the equivalent of ten to twelve ordinary lorry tanker loads, and would only need a crew of two, rather than an individual driver for each vehicle.

The glassworks was demolished in 1988 and was replaced by the Novotel Hotel. The works had actually closed in December 1983, and in 1984 a 200-bedroomed hotel was proposed, along with 120 houses and flats on the site. A restaurant and pub were also suggested, but these did not materialise.

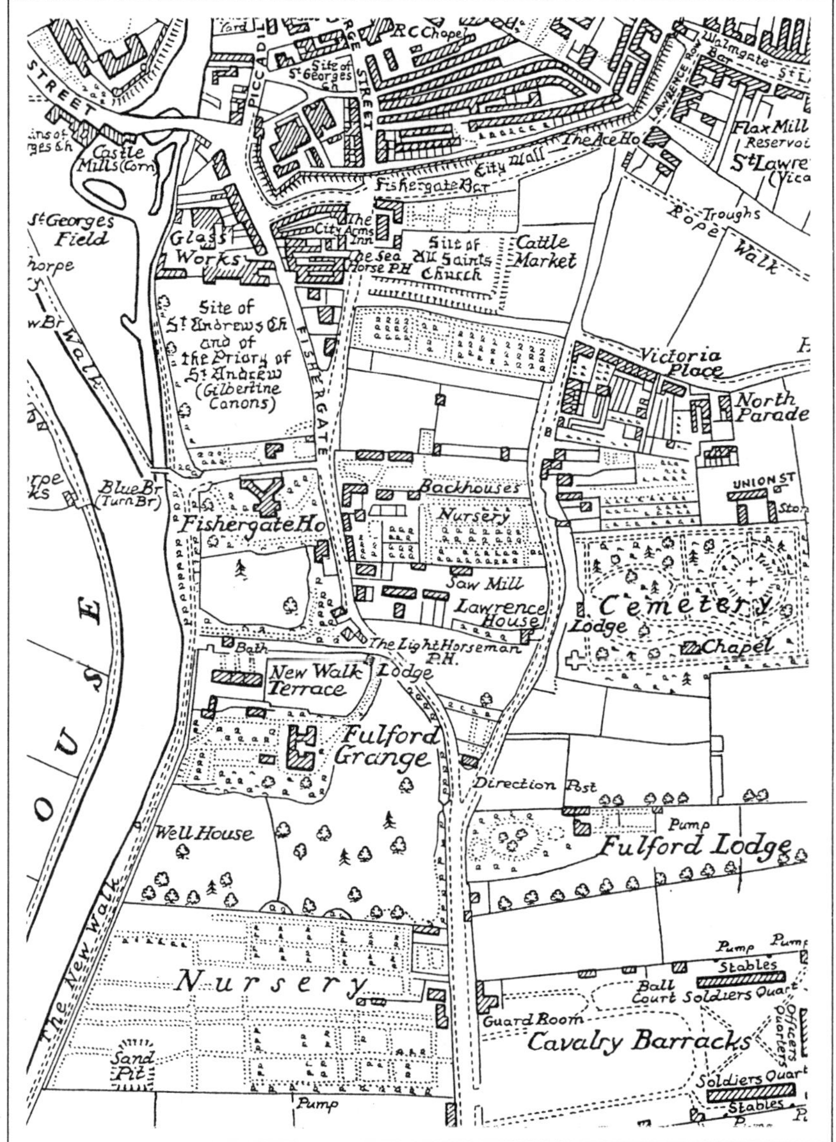

Fishergate and Fulford Road, 1849

In 1986, York Archaeological Trust excavated the site, and discovered not only parts of the medieval Gilbertine Priory, but also, beneath that, remains of 8th Century York, which was named Eoforwic. Traces of a small timber church and cemetery were found, which were of 9th-10th century, and it was thought that this had been replaced by a stone church of the Norman period, which was used as a basis for the Priory. The church must have been the Parish Church of St Andrew, owned by Newburgh Priory. The building was extended and adapted as a monastery.

During the dig, over 10,000 small finds were unearthed, including early pencils and 'parchment pickers (an early form of plotting lines for writing), pottery, weights, bone knives, fragments of glass vessels, and quernstones which had been used for grinding flour (and were introduced to England by the Roman army). There were also pieces of window glass which were fitted together, and found to be examples of Germanic art. A plan was made of the Priory, siting each of the areas, such as dormitories, refectory and cloister, and it was concluded that rebuilding had taken place in the mid 14th century. During the excavation, several of the archaeologists reported sitings of a ghost walking along the gantry overhead, possibly on the site of the old dormitories.

The glassworks did not occupy the whole site of the Gilbertine Priory, as the map of 1849 shows. Just beyond the works was the open land of Stone Wall Close. In 1895 there were also the York Sewerage Works and the Sewerage Works Mission Room. Today, the newly built road leading down from Fishergate to the hotel is called Fewster Way, named after Ebenezer Fewster who became Ouse Navigation River manager in March 1923. He was chosen out of 203 applicants, and stayed for 22 years, being succeeded in 1945 by his son, William Drysdale Fewster, who died in August 1960. Father and son had served 37 years with the company between them.

8

Work for Women

One of the most significant buildings for women in the area was the Wenlock Laundry, situated in Ambrose Street. The York Public Laundry had been the first laundry in the street, and in April 1881 the Gazette reported that an 'experienced laundress from Jersey has been engaged'. She was Alice Hirst, wife of Henry Hirst, an unemployed printer. The Wenlock Laundry, designed by G T Fowler Jones, was built for Mr T C Johnson in October 1896 at 61-75 Ambrose Street. In the basement were two large cellars for stores, five small cellars and a coalhouse. On the ground floor was a large washhouse with a skylight above, a smaller drying room, a small office, living room, drying closets, fuel store, scullery and larder and only two wc's. On the first floor was a large packing room with three ironing rooms, two iron-heating rooms and three small bedrooms. From 1901 the laundry was extended to include numbers 59 to 61. The business tended to cater largely for the wealthy families of Fulford and Naburn. Mrs Florence Fenn, whose mother worked at the laundry, remembers being taken to help out there,

When I was eight they used to stand me on a little flat basket, 'cos I couldn't reach the table very well. I used to iron all the handkerchiefs, every one.

The handkerchieves were linen, finely embroidered with sheets of pink and mauve paper inserted between each one. The laundry provided employment for many women in the area. There were at least twelve women to iron, half a dozen in the washhouse and four on the calender.

Mrs Fenn describes it,

a great long thing which the sheets used to go through. Never used to iron sheets, used to put 'em through the calender.

On Saturday evenings, the tingalarie man toured the streets with his monkey. The women from the laundry would come out after their tea, and dance in Ambrose Street as he played all the well-known songs of the day. It was the highlight of their week, a week which often saw them at work from 8 am to 8 pm when business was booming, before they returned home to yet more domestic chores.

In September 1913 the Laundry saw its first strike. It had become part of the Yorkshire Laundries Ltd, and all the city's laundries, both steam and hand, came out on strike for a period of ten days, demanding a standard rate of wages and hours. Picketing was 'carried out in a peaceful and persuasive manner which constitutes law and order' stated the Gazette. On Saturday 4th October a settlement was reached between the laundry proprietors and the workers' representatives, at a conference at the Station Hotel, where a wage of 12s a week was agreed upon. (Fortunately, strike pay had been received from the National Federation of Women Workers.) This was four days after a huge demonstration in the city market place where the York City band turned out to entertain the crowds.

In 1919 the laundry was renamed the Riverside Laundry and Dyeworks, part of Robert Abbot and Son, a company of art dyers, dry cleaners and laundrymen, whose other branches were located at Coney Street and Micklegate.

By 1929 the laundry had closed down, being replaced by Binns & McAdam Vulcanisers and Tyre Factors. In the early 1930s the property was separated into two buildings - Summers & Barnes organ builders in one, and the Poultry Food Supply Company which manufactured cereal foods, was based in the other. Children in the area enjoyed their first taste of macaroni there, as it lay in sacks waiting to be hoisted by crane into the granary and store rooms above. In 1950, Rees and Gee metal and machinery merchants took the lease, later giving way to Nevison-Shepherd furniture manufacturers, and in the 1960s, York Removals Ltd.

York Removals (once Wenlock Laundry), 1984

In January 1970 there was a huge fire at the premises, the damage from which was estimated at thousands of pounds. Two bricklayers working outside escaped unhurt, and the couple next door had to be evacuated. The whole street turned out to watch as thirty firemen with nine jets, seven fire engines from York Fire Brigade, Tadcaster, Easingwold and Rowntrees Fire Service, attacked the blazing building. Two women from the Ordnance Depot canteen and several neighbours brought tea for the firemen, who managed to save the premises.

In 1990 the old building was demolished and eight new houses were built there by W A Hare, incorporating bricks from the original buildings. The new houses are in the early Victorian style and are numbered 61 to 73.

As well as the official laundry, many local women took in washing for the barracks, to supplement their meagre incomes. Ken Richmond from Frances Street describes his mother's work during the period of economic depression following the First World War,

She used to take washing in. And I used to have a barrow and take it in to the barracks. She used to wash solid for three days and then iron for three days. All night as well sometimes. She used to have an old copper and an old wooden mangle. It had like a cradle on it. Inside it was like a round drum, all wood across, wood laths, you used to put your washing in and then turn the handle, saved a lot of peggying. There were starched collars in them days and she only had an old gas iron and there used to be flames shooting out of this gas iron. It was a bit deadly! Most of 'em did the washing out in their back yards in them days, their scrubbing you know. She used to charge a penny for a towel, shirts were about - the grey-backed shirts, old soldier's shirts, I think they were tuppence - and fancy shirts as they called them were threepence. Socks were a penny.

Mr Kent's mother also took in soldiers' laundry,

Each man's bundle was rolled up. Shirt, vest, pants and socks. Each man had to pay sevenpence, that's all she got. She boiled them in coal copper and scrubbed them on the kitchen table. She had to fasten a tape on each article with the name on. I had to stay up late helping, and write the names on the tapes.

For most women, life was very difficult during the depression, and Millie Fenn tells of how some women could not cope with the drudgery of their lives. One woman from Frances Street threw her baby into the river, and one or two others committed suicide by jumping into the water. Another lady retreated into madness. Her husband worked at the flour mill and while he was out, she would destroy items in the home, finally setting the bed on fire. She was eventually committed to an asylum, and the street turned out to watch as,

four policemen took her off in a taxi. She wouldn't go, she knocked their helmets off.

Another organisation run by women, was founded in the late 1970s. The Ladderback Co-operative was housed in the basement of number 3 Wenlock Terrace, once servant quarters. It was a registered workers' co-operative, one of six in York, employing four women, Mary Raw (now Lewis), Rosemary Hawksford, Pennie Hamer and Sue Reeves, to repair cane and rush furniture, and traditional upholstery, and to repair and renovate wood. The business was run on the underlying principles of conservation and recycling. The women enjoyed the sense of working with natural products. They fixed their own hours and paid themselves equal wages, and because all had children, the co-operative paid their nursery fees. Mary explains,

We know we are working for each other so we share the responsibilities and decisions, we decide what our holidays should be, what hours we should work and who is going to do a particular job.

The co-operative opened from 10am to 4pm Tuesday to Saturday, and in addition the members travelled to craft fairs and agricultural shows. Their large workroom retained its original black kitchen range, and a smaller room adjacent (the servants' scullery) had a small range and old copper. In the pantry were large storage shelves which would once have kept food cold before the invention of refrigerators. On the first floor, the rooms were connected by inner doors with red and blue leaded glass etched in starred patterns, and floors of inlaid mosaic, so that the whole house retained a Victorian ambience.

9

Education and the Church

Today there are several schools in the Fishergate area. Fishergate Primary School, St George's Catholic primary, and in Fulford Cross is the Steiner School. The oldest is Fishergate, a typical Victorian school, which was designed by Demaine and Brierley and opened in 1895, on the site of St Helen's Church, which was demolished by Act of Parliament in 1547. Walter Brierley was also responsible for the National Westminster Bank on the corner of New Street, Holy Trinity Rectory in Micklegate and the Burton Stone Inn, but his work is seen mostly on various York schools. Park Grove, Haxby Road, Poppleton Road, Scarcroft and Acomb are some examples. The roof of Fishergate School has two bell towers, and originally had two separate entrances, like many other schools of the period, one for boys, and one for girls.

In the 1950s and 1960s it was the venue for the eleven-plus examinations for most of the York primary schools, being the largest and most central. Last year the school celebrated its centenary, with an exhibition of photographs and memorabilia, and the production of a history of the school. The school is certainly remembered with affection by its ex-pupils, although the discipline was very strict in the early days. Helen Wildon experienced this,

I loved learning and I loved school, I wasn't struck on holidays. I was going to school one day and it was pouring with rain, and I was running by. And there was a man on a ladder washing some windows, it was a public house, and it struck lightning and this man dropped off the ladder. I heard the crash and he was dead. It upset me that much, I thought 'If I'm late I'll get the stick'.

You always got the stick if you were a minute late. But I thought I'd better go and tell them in this pub. So I told this woman and she said 'Sit down a minute' and I'm sure she gave me a drop of brandy, though I said I don't drink. They offered to take me to school but I said 'No I'd better go'. When I got there, the teacher said, 'Have you seen the time?' and wouldn't let me explain. She brought the cane out and gave me a stroke, and I pulled my hand back so it didn't come down too hard, so she gave me another and then another.

I sat in the class and all of a sudden I started to cry, from shock. She said, 'Would you like to sit outside?' I sat on a chair outside and our headmaster Mr Barker came round and said, 'What's matter with you?' so I told him, and he said he'd never heard anything so horrible in his life. And he went in there and shouted at that teacher, and said, 'She didn't need to come to school but she came to school and look at the reception she got'.

Ken Richmond's class, Fishergate School, c1930

Ken Richmond was another victim of corporal punishment,

The arithmetic teacher as they were then, they used to call him Icky Rason. He was a First World War officer, he didn't have a cane, he had a calla, piece of flat wood. Used to get it across your bottom. If he was in a bad humour he'd lay it on a bit heavy.

But Fishergate encouraged a wide range of subjects and sometimes pupils ventured elsewhere for activities, as Ken remembers,

We used to go for metalwork to Haxby Road school and you got a free ride on t'tram there and back. I think everybody made a toasting fork in them days. It was the only thing he could trust us with. Now and then they used to take us round historic parts of York on a Saturday morning, took us to t'top of Cliffords Tower once, there's only one wall at one side and then a flat piece, scared us all to death.

Ken Richmond also remembers playing cricket in the schoolyard,

One time I was batting and the teacher says to me, 'For goodness sake, lad, open your shoulders and hit it'. I did and it went right through t'window!

Another ex-pupil recalls a teacher named Mr Lambert,

He had a degree in nature studies. He had a large bunch of arum lilies, and I'd never seen any before except on top of a coffin. He gave a lily to every child in the class, and under his direction we pulled 'em all to pieces to see the stamens and pistils, and we got to know how a flower was constructed.

Mrs Close remembers going to dances at the school,

It was sixpence and everybody used to go in a long dress. And we used to dance to records, on a wind-up gramophone. It used to start about seven o'clock and finish at ten and you used to think it was grand. Everybody used to get dressed

up to the nines to go to a dance, now they go in jeans. We had silver shoes, we used to think we were the cat's whiskers.

St George's Primary had originally been in Margaret Street, off Walmgate, and the new premises in Fishergate were only opened in 1977. The site, in Winterscale Street, is that of the medieval St Helen's Church and nearby leper hospital. The new school opened on the Feast of St Vincent de Paul, 27th of September.

The governors and staff had been petitioning for a new school for some years, primarily because the old one was lacking in facilities. There were no playing fields, no gymnasium and not enough sinks, for one thing. Yet, as Mr Atkin who was deputy head, explains,

It was always friendly, a happy cheerful place. At the old school, the people there were very happy, but obviously they were delighted to go into the new school because nobody's going to complain if they get brand new equipment and better facilities. I think the spirit of the school transferred, that wasn't lost. Mainly because it was the same group of teachers who transferred, it was just the building that changed. The important thing, the people, didn't change.

The Sisters of Charity of St Vincent de Paul had taught at the school for many years, in the capacity of head teacher, and the last nun to teach there was Sister Mary, who retired in 1985. She was replaced by the present head, a lay teacher, Mr Norman Fowler, who is also, in his spare time, the singer Steve Cassidy.

The Steiner School in Fulford Cross had originally been in Bishophill Senior and is relatively new in this area. It occupies the old Danesmead School. The school regularly holds one-day fairs open to the public, with a range of music, activities and events available.

The Church and the Mission Rooms

St Oswald's church on Main Street, Fulford, is the parish church for the area, but at the end of the 19th century, a satellite for the church opened nearer to Fishergate.

Alma Terrace has always been part of the parish. In 1873 the Fulford Parish magazine reported that the church had begun a series of cottage lectures in the village on Tuesday evenings. The Vicar told his parishioners,

"If we could find a suitable room we should like to carry on a similar work in Alma Terrace on Thursday evenings. No doubt when the time comes, 'a door will be opened unto us' in this populous district and we shall be able to establish a weekly service, as witness for God in its midst."

The Rev Henry Farrow, Vicar of Fulford, went on to express his concern for the area in the Parish Magazine of August 1878,

"There is one part of the parish which is beginning to cause us some anxiety for the future. It is that part lying opposite to the Barrack gates. Plans have been drawn and we believe much of the property sold in lots of 240 new houses of about £10 p.a. rental to form two streets running from the high road to the river ... How to meet the educational and spiritual wants of these people is a problem we shall soon be called upon to solve. At present it seems to us not too early to secure an eligible site in the centre of the property on which at some time an iron church might be put as preparatory to a more permanent building."

By September 1878 a house had been found in Alma Terrace where cottage lectures began every Thursday evening at 7.30 pm, conducted by laymen in conjunction with the clergy. A year later, the lectures proving successful, a room 'in that rapidly increasing district for the purpose of a Sunday school and week-night service is sadly needed'.

The first Mission Room, named St Andrew's (probably because St Andrew's Priory had occupied the land between Fishergate and New Walk from 1202 to 1538) was founded in 1880 at 29 Frances Street, for which the church paid £10 a year rent. Meetings were held each Thursday, and on 8th July 1880 the Vicar was granted, by the Archbishop of York, a licence to officiate. On Christmas Day there was an early morning celebration of Holy Communion, in January 1881 the first two baptisms took place, and in February confirmation classes began. Another addition to the weekly programme was the Monday temperance meeting, which ended with the provision of soup. At this time too, donations began to arrive for the Lending Library and Reading Room. By March 1891, the Mission Room was really flourishing. The following meetings were held regularly,

Sunday	Holy Communion (2nd in month)	8 am
	Sunday School	2.30 pm
	Men's Bible Class	4 pm
	Evensong with sermon	6.30 pm
Thursday	Special Mission service with address	8 pm

The Mission was run by Rev Frederick Chambers of Howard Street, assistant curate to the Vicar, Rev Windham Beresford Peirse. March saw a series of sermons by Mr Chambers on the life and work of Jesus Christ as foretold in the Old Testament, under the headings of: The Innocent Sufferer, Message of Forgiveness and Hope of Salvation.

In August of that year, the Mission Choir had their annual outing to Scarborough. Eighteen members travelled by train and had an enjoyable day despite pouring rain, managing to find refuge in the Aquarium and

St Nicholas' Restaurant. The following month there was an appeal for more books for the lending library, after complaints that members had read all the existing copies and that these were beginning to show definite signs of wear and tear. The appeal requested 'any storybooks of a suitable character or other entertaining and instructive volumes', and stressed that the givers would have 'the happiness of feeling that they are helping others to devote their leisure hours to a pleasant and profitable occasion'.

The satellite church continued to expand, and by the start of 1898 there were two additions to the weekly programme, the Mothers' Meeting and a branch of the Fulford clothing club. By May, enough donations had been received to purchase a harmonium for the Church services. It soon became apparent that a small house was not adequate to continue the service which the Mission provided. In 1893 plans had begun to build a Mission Church, and a piece of land was acquired measuring 403 square yards from Mrs Elizabeth Abbey in Alma Terrace. Walter Brierley, the renowned York architect, was commissioned to design the new church which would, when complete, accommodate 217 adults. At first the plans proved to be too elaborate and expensive, but once they had been modified and the cost lowered, building went into operation, carried out by G & L Lough of Blyth. The house adjoining the Mission (61 Alma Terrace) became the caretaker's residence.

On 10th November 1900 a ceremony was held to lay the foundation stone of the new Mission Rooms. The clergy and choir were permitted to robe in the Police Station, from which the procession began at 3 pm. The Bishop of Beverley conducted the service and the stone was laid by G T Faber, MP, in the presence of the Lord Mayor and other city officials. The building was licensed but not consecrated; public worship and baptisms were permitted but not weddings or funerals. The main room had an altar and a vestry, with a Parish Room and Boys' Club Room beyond.

In the 1940s, St Andrew's Church Council was formed as an advisory committee to the Parish Church Council. The Rooms were also leased out for other functions such as parties and wedding receptions. Ken Richmond attended regularly,

That used to be the Sunday School. You used to 'ave to go on Sunday afternoons, and, well, you tried to jig it, but I couldn't because my auntie taught there.

Mrs Nancy Dawson was rather more enthusiastic,

If they wanted to hold a church [service] there was two rooms and if they wanted to hold a sale of work, as long as they covered the altar up across, with a curtain, they could use the rest of the room. It was Harvest festival and they used to have the afternoon one where the kiddies all sang and then one at night. I forget what I was singing but the organist was an old gentleman. All my brothers and their wives went to see, you'd to stand up on this form and sing, and all he had to do was give me the note. Well he went all wrong and I sat down and I couldn't sing anymore and I wept. Of course my brothers said, 'I'm not going to listen to 'er sing anymore, she's hopeless, she cries'. My mother had arranged to go at night so she had a word with the organist's daughter, who said, 'Don't worry I'm playing tonight'. She gave me the right note and I sang it. Me mother was so chuffed because I'd sang it right through.

I always remember all I ever wanted was a real baby doll. We went to the sale of work and there was one there and somebody had dressed it. It was beautiful, all in white-lace dress and shawl, and you'd to guess the name of the doll. I said, 'Oh I'd like that doll, mummy' and she said, 'Well, we'll have to guess'. They were guessing Penelopes and all sorts of fancy names and me mother said, 'Ann. Plain Ann, I want no e on the end'. And I won the doll, that made my day. They had originally been farmers you see so they were real plain people, didn't want no fancy names, Ann or nothing at all.

Mrs Dawson also enjoyed being a part of Fulford church itself, especially at Christmas,

We used to go singing with the young curate. He was married with two kids, and half of the meetings were at the house. Then my sister in law and a neighbour used to make hot coffee and hot mince pies and we'd go singing all round Fulford and Fulford Road area. Then we'd end up about eleven o'clock back at these homes for coffee and mince pies, and then all go en masse to Holy Communion at midnight.

Mr Ron Sheppeard recalls other uses of the Mission Hall,

They formed the CLB - Church Lads' Brigade, and Junior Training Corps and there was a girls' equivalent. It was run by a man called Eddie Johnson. We used to pay a penny a week subs, and we used to go there for boxing. I used to write plays and we used to perform them on the stage there. It was nice and warm, it was somewhere to go. They had dances on a Saturday night. You could always get a band because the West Yorkshire Band was stationed at the Barracks.

Another local lady remembers the dances there too,

We never went to an army dance, me Dad wouldn't have allowed it. We used to go to a little place down Alma Terrace, and a lot of soldiers used to go there, it was a 'tanner hop'. Sometimes you'd see somebody you thought you'd like.

The last service to be held there was on 25th April 1954, when eighteen communicants met for evensong. Sunday School continued until 22nd September 1957 with a regular gathering of between thirty and forty. In 1959 the building was leased to Greenhills wholesale drapers, and then in 1969 to L C Oliver the wholesale hotel suppliers. Today the Mission Rooms have been demolished and replaced by four new properties, numbers 53 to 59.

For such a heavily-populated area, it is unusual to find no other churches between Fulford village and Walmgate. In 1883 the Salvation Army established a second corps in Fawcett Street, off Fishergate. General Booth, the Army's founder, even appeared there to address a meeting in that year. But the Corps moved to premises vacated by the Wesleyan North Street Mission in 1905.

Mission Rooms Coronation Party 1953

10

Epidemics and Petitions

In November 1892 there was great concern in both Frances Street and Ambrose Street when an epidemic of typhoid broke out. Oliver Hallett, a lodger at 58 Frances Street, was the first to die. The jury at the inquest expressed the opinion that rubbish thrown in the back lanes was unhealthy, and that the Corporation should undertake the cleansing and purifying of the privies at frequent intervals. The Council stepped in and instructed house owners in both streets to replace privies and ashpits with proper toilets, and thus improve sanitary conditions. On 4th May 1891 a child died in a house in Frances Street due to overcrowding. There were two rooms on the ground floor which housed a couple with four children, and on the floor above lived another couple and their three young children. The Medical Officer of Health inspected the house and instructed that numbers be reduced, presumably by one family moving out.

In 1903 there was an outbreak of scarlet fever in the city, which also had fatal results, affecting Alma Terrace and Frances Street. Disease was rife at this period, frequently because of poor sanitation and overcrowding, and the under-nourishment of the working class. Though the area was by no means a slum, house owners did not seem willing to go to the expense of improving conditions, and often had to be cajoled by the Corporation.

Over the course of a hundred years, this area has seen its share of petitions from the residents. In February 1888 the Council received a petition signed by 141 persons who were residents and rate payers of

Frances Street, 'praying for the removal of the wall at the end of that street, which prevents the inhabitants of that district having access to the New Walk'. The Council appeared to be sympathetic to the complaint, but had to negotiate with the residents of Holly Terrace which faced the river. The petition stated that,

> 1. The original arrangement of streets included a direct way from Frances Street onto the New Walk, and that a part, at least, of the property, was purchased under that implied condition.
>
> 2. That the land, which is now shut off as private land, has already been held to be a part of the public road, and a public lamp has been fixed upon it.
>
> 3. That the present open doorway at the foot of Ambrose Street left open at the sufferance of the owners of Holly Terrace, is not convenient for the residents of Frances Street, being further from the town than that street.

But the occupants of Holly Terrace were angry that their property should be considered a 'right of way'. They claimed that payment of an annual acknowledgement to the Council, however minimal, gave them exclusive access onto the New Walk. A further petition signed by 157 persons, was submitted in October 1890. The Council's Estates Committee investigated, but the result remained the same.

Whilst the Frances Street occupants were still campaigning for access to the riverside, something occurred to close the Ambrose Street access too. The occupier of 8 Holly Terrace sent an irate letter to the Council in April 1925 complaining that a football had broken a plate glass window in his house, and he felt compelled to move because his family were afraid to use the dining room, drawing room or kitchen. A week later he dispatched a further missive stating that he had had 'several narrow escapes this week'. A party of councillors arrived to inspect the access, and discovered that the gate leading to the river was closed, and a note posted to the effect that it would remain so. A huge petition, this time signed by residents from Ambrose Street, Frances Street, Alma Terrace, Wenlock Terrace, Fulford Road and other streets further afield was submitted to the Council in protest, stating that the roadway had been in common use for over thirty years. The councillors also noted that the Frances Street access was permanently closed. It seemed incomprehensible to the inhabitants that although there was a flight of steps leading from New Walk to the foot of their street, access was restricted to occupiers of Holly Terrace. After seeing the situation for themselves, the councillors prevailed upon the Streets and Buildings Committee to use their influence to ensure that the doorway be kept open for public use. The owners denied this request.

Then a third letter from 8 Holly Terrace informed the Council that 'a controversy is at present raging in my neighbourhood'. The occupier claimed that when he witnessed soldiers urinating outside his house, this was the last straw. He also accused the local children of being rowdy and their parents of doing little to dissuade them from bad behaviour, but instead 'taking every opportunity to peer in at the windows and taunt myself and my wife'.

The Council was placed in a somewhat difficult position, but they managed to satisfy both sides by arranging to purchase a piece of vacant land adjoining 12 Holly Terrace, in January 1926. Then they had the footpath made up on the south side of the private road and extended the steps in line with this footpath onto the New Walk, so that it could be used as public access. The vacant land was offered to the Housing Committee for the purpose of erecting new houses, but the offer at that time was declined. In July 1928 the land remaining vacant, the residents of Ambrose Street petitioned the Council to allow children to use it as a playground, there being no suitable play area in the vicinity. Despite objections from Holly Terrace, the Council complied with the request, on condition that the age of the children should not exceed twelve years.

The play area was colloquially referred to as the 'Hen Run' because one local tenant kept some hens in a corner, fenced off by barbed wire. Hens were not uncommon in the area, and several people in Alma Terrace kept livestock, because their gardens were quite long, reaching as far as Farndale Street on the Grange estate. Rabbits and chickens were also popular. The Hen Run was used by all the children in the area, and Ken Richmond gives his version of the incident which led to the complaints,

It had just a wicker door at one end. And course you were always losing balls in either Ordnance or breaking doo-dah's window. When summat like that happened, we all used to scoot straight off over the wall. One of the lads kicked the football and it went through t'window, and landed in his breakfast. Anyway he came out and pinched all our coats which we'd left for goalposts, took 'em all in his house and he took us all to court. We all got fined tuppence each It broke a vase actually and he reckoned it was worth a lot of money, but I don't think it was, it was a cheap vase. I think it upset his breakfast, that's what he was most bothered about.

The popularity of this playground and its importance in people's memories can be summed up in these two comments,

If ever there was a fight, if someone threatened somebody, it was always in the Hen Run they had this fight. Before long instead of two fighting, there were about twenty two. (Ken Richmond)

The Hen Run was our Stadium. That was our Wembley and our Lord's and everybody played there. (Ron Sheppeard)

In recent years, as traffic has become an increasingly large problem in York, and especially in narrow streets like these, the residents have campaigned for some means of slowing down vehicles. In Summer 1989, a local parent collected 200 signatures on a petition for sleeping policemen to be installed in the lane linking Frances Street and Ambrose

Street. The petition was reported in the Yorkshire Evening Press, and local children were interviewed on Radio York; then local councillor John Boardman (Lord Mayor in 1995) and Labour Party press officer Hugh Bayley (now York's MP) presented the petition to the council, but the problem has still not been dealt with. There have been near misses involving children, and cars are getting faster all the time, but it will probably take a serious accident to get some action.

Also in the summer of 1989, there was another drama in Frances Street, which echoed the earlier petitions and contretemps about the right of way. The owners of the two houses on Holly Terrace, at the bottom of Frances Street, had some building work done, which included the demolition of garages, fences and gates. This left the way open to the steps onto New Walk. People began to use the land as a right of way, believing that it was now public property, and when the owners of the two houses questioned this, arguments ensued. The Evening Press reported that 'two York households have suffered abuse, vandalism and theft since giving fellow residents a chance to walk through their courtyards'. One householder, Mary Saldhana, put up a sign stating 'private' but this was painted out more than once, and even stolen. Eventually, a whole chapter of graffiti was painted onto the end wall, though the culprit was never found.

11

Leisure Time

As far as leisure is concerned, the main sources in this area were the Rialto and the pubs. The Rialto started life as the City Roller Skating Rink in Fishergate in 1908/9. Sydney Bacon secured the site on Mollett's field, and the rink was built. It was made of corrugated iron with a stone frontage, a floor of rock maple, and erected under canvas, claiming to be 'the largest tent ever erected', lit by electricity and decorated with banners. The tent was only temporary, whilst a permanent building was erected around it. The skating pavilion was formally opened in May 1909 by the Lord Mayor, James Birch.

City Skating Rink, 1909

In August 1910, a season of 'alfresco' variety concerts began to be held there, under the direction of Mr K Scott Barrie. On opening night, the artistes began the entertainment by singing 'Come and see the show', a phrase echoed ever since! This was followed by songs rendered by Mr P Howley, Mr Jack Kenyon and Miss Dalton, whilst Mr Charles Armstrong 'applied a capital store of humour'. Prices ranged from 3d to 1s.

During 1912 there were several matches of five-a-side roller rink hockey at the rink. York had a good team and were in the national league. The teams were smaller than the usual six-man ice hockey teams, and usually composed of four or five. In 1913 the rink was divided into two, and the front section became a cinema whilst skating continued at the rear. During the First World War the premises were used for military billets. A dancing licence was granted in October 1925.

In 1928 the place moved into a new era, with the arrival of John Xavier (Jack) Prendergast. He converted the skating rink into a ballroom, and in 1929 it was renamed the Rialto Cinema and Ballroom, the first York cinema to show talkies in July of that year. In 1935 the building (both cinema and ballroom) was destroyed by fire, with damage estimated at £30,000. Fishergate was filled with clouds of smoke, but fortunately no-one was injured. Fire engines rushed to the scene at 5.30 in the morning, the trailer pump was taken down to the river and firemen fought for two hours to put out the blaze. A witness described the scene as 'an inferno, with flames forty-foot high'. Amazingly, the Rialto was completely rebuilt by November, when it re-opened with the film 'Gold Diggers of 1935'.

Ken Richmond went to the cinema as a boy,

Used to have roller skating on one night a week. Once or twice we used to get a ticket and go in to t'cinema when we left school at four o'clock. We stopped there and saw it twice through, the talkie had just come in.

Rialto Souvenir

Mrs Close also went along,

It was a roller skating rink, called the 'Casino' and it had a sort of tarpaulin roof. If you weren't careful and it was raining, you got wet. I've seen people sitting with umbrellas in there. There was a dance hall at the side. You could pay to go and roller skate, and you could sit and watch them skating and for sixpence, I think you got a cup of tea and a biscuit as well. We used to go to the pictures as children and it was three pence. And they used to give you a bar of chocolate or toffee. In the bar of toffee there used to be perhaps one stamp of one part of the picture. When you got it completed you took your picture in and you got another big slab of toffee.

Cycle Races, Rialto, 1930s

June Lloyd-Jones, daughter of Mr Prendergast, describes the place,

The main feature was the Spanish dancer, and the lattice work. There was a veranda round, and you could go upstairs and have coffee and drinks. The downstairs was a beautiful wooden sprung floor. I think there were settees round, and I remember they used to have roller skating, and other things quite apart from the dances. And they used to have these funny little cycle races. Can you imagine doing that in evening dress? And Dad with the starting gun.

One lady who regularly attended, remembers,

We used to go to the City Picture Palace, and half way down the seats were cheaper. We used to go in the cheaper seats and then when t'attendants had gone, we used to keep shifting a bit further back till we got in t'back seats. Then we could do a bit of canoodling.

Cinemas closed for a week at the beginning of the Second World War, but re-opened on September 11th 1939, when the Rialto showed Ronald Colman in 'The Masquerader' accompanied by Bela Lugosi in 'The White Zombie' as an example of sheer escapism. The cinema advertised air raid shelters only fifty yards away and also had an anti air-raid gun on the roof. Edward Farley, the popular organist at the Rialto, also played at Clifton Cinema and would race down in a taxi from one place to the other, though legend also had it that he would jump on his bicycle to get there quickly. Farley had played the organ in Canterbury Cathedral at the age of thirteen, and was the youngest regular church organist at fourteen. In 1921 he began to play in cinemas, and came to York in 1937 from a residency at the Astoria in Brixton, and married Miss Great Britain 1936. He composed songs to commemorate York City's five cup run of 1937-8, when they reached the sixth round. He left York in 1940, succeeded by Horace Pilling, and became organist at the Odeon in Leeds, then organist-manager at the Regal in Bridlington, followed by the Ritz in Lincoln. He returned to York in 1944 and whilst at the Regal, in Piccadilly, he put on a big patriotic concert with over 130 members of the forces with him on stage. He left again in 1949, and died suddenly whilst playing in Broadstairs in 1962.

Mrs Betty Thompson remembers,

We used to go to the Rialto, Edward Farley on the organ. And he played for half an hour and we used to have to sing all these songs but it was all worded. It was wartime and we used to sing 'Roll out the Barrel' and all those wartime songs, and songs from the past and sheets with the words on.

Both the Rialto and Clifton Cinema belonged to Mr Prendergast who lived at Fulford House. When he opened Clifton, the programme stated that 'his endeavour will be to amuse, thrill, enchant, foster the human sympathies and leave all patrons with a feeling that the evening has not been wasted'. Those who frequented the two places would agree with these sentiments.

Prendergast House, Fulford Road
(now the Pavilion Hotel)

Jack Prendergast was a well-known figure in York. As his daughter recalls, he was also a warm-up man at the Rialto concerts,

Dad used to come on at the beginning and tell a few jokes, and he had to be good to start with. He became a very good joke teller.

Born in 1898, Prendergast began his career as manager of the Palladium in Lancaster. In 1940 he was commandant of the Auxiliary Fire Service in York, and later became chairman of the Cinematograph Exhibition Association. His son Barry became the composer John Barry. Barry was musical director of the show 'Oh Boy' in 1959 and won his first gold disc for the music from the James Bond film, 'Goldfinger', in 1965 and his first Oscar for the soundtrack of 'Born Free' in 1967, followed a year later by another Oscar for best original film score with 'The Lion in Winter'. In 1985, his music for 'Out of Africa' won another Academy Award, as did his soundtrack of Kevin Costner's 'Dances with Wolves' in 1990.

Beside the cinema was the Rialto Sweet Shop, run by Mrs Prendergast, which Ken Richmond also visited,

She used to give you some peanuts and some broken chocolate for a ha'penny.

June Lloyd-Jones recalls one man who came in for Woodbines,

We kept the packet for him under the counter and he came in and used to buy a single Woodbine at a time, half-penny or three-halfpenny.

From 1930, the shops in the same block as the Rialto became known as Rialto Buildings, and included a chemist, dairy, jeweller and decorator. At the other side of the sweet shop was Tramways Club and Institute. This had moved in the late 1920s from its base at Phoenix House on Castle Mills Bridge, and by 1970 it had moved again, to Mill Street, off Piccadilly.

Rialto Programme

The Rialto was also used for what were known as the St Patrick's Day concerts. Tom Rhodes remembers them,

We used to have them once a year. You were selected out for different dances or singing and what have you. The Rialto was Fishergate cinema and John Prendergast bought it and big Catholic family, he was friendly with the priest, and he used to let us have this. We did used to get a little suit, I had to rely on me grandmother, bought me a new suit. You had to have a bow and all that, the money went between St George's and St Wilfrid's and I think they gave English Martyrs so much out of it. They had one or two good artists of a kind.

During the war, Prendergast arranged Sunday night shows for the forces, who were allowed in for 6d, whereas any civilian would pay a shilling.

In the late 1930s and 1940s, as more cinemas appeared in York, the Rialto became more popular as a venue for live entertainment, having its own swing band, Len Cundall (who played double bass) and the Rialtonians. (The band lost some of its instruments in the 1935 fire, but were able to replace them before too long.) Another popular 'big band' was the Embassy Band. Saturday night was dance night, when the dance floor would resound to the tunes of the tango, foxtrot, quickstep, valeta and waltz.

Eileen Brown enjoyed the dances there,

Everybody in York knew the Prendergasts. The father was a lovely big man and I knew the boys as they were coming up. On New Year's Eve he used to have a dance that didn't start until midnight, until the next day. And you all went round the Minster when the bells were ringing the old year out and the New Year in.

I was never short of dancing partners. You didn't dance in your outdoor shoes, you always had dance shoes with you. My mother was a dressmaker. I could buy a piece of material Saturday morning and she could make a dress for me, Saturday night, and they used to be drooping backs or four corners long. My mother was a lovely dressmaker, I allus had something new.

Over the years, the Rialto featured many international acts including American stars Louis Armstrong, Sarah Vaughan, Johnny Mathis, the Everley Brothers, the Inkspots and Stan Kenton and his Orchestra.

June Lloyd-Jones remembers,

It was huge. It was a beautiful ballroom. All the big functions were held in the ballroom because it was probably the largest venue in York. Hal Fielding was the agent, and got a lot of these people. There was never to my knowledge a contract signed, it was all done on a handshake, I think it was tremendous, the fact that business can be done like that.

One firm favourite was Gracie Fields, a personal friend of the Prendergasts.

They went and stayed with her in Capri when she had her home there. I think Daddy had met her in the early days, and that friendship had carried on. She says on the photograph, something about, 'My coming to York is one of the highlights of my tour'. I think it's just because it's like coming back to friends.

The cinema side continued, of course, and Prendergast, being an independent, could choose his own films.

Dad was fairly experimental, in that he liked to show foreign films. We did do a series of late-night Saturday nights, where we showed excellent foreign films, so we had a huge backing. In that area when there was nothing else available and other people weren't prepared to show them.

But the standard films were the most popular and in the summer of 1947, when they showed Bob Hope in 'The Paleface',

We had queues from the Rialto down to St George's baths. We were an eighteen hundred seater and we were packed every performance.

Going to the cinema wasn't just a matter of seeing a film. There was more to it, as June Lloyd-Jones recalls,

I think people liked the singalong, it set the atmosphere. You used to go in at half-past six or seven and get a real good double feature, the second feature was a good film as well. Then you got your news reel. You got a good night out, a full programme, it was value for money in those days.

Queues at the Rialto

Comfort was also important,

We had a front balcony - half a crown, that was your top price, in comfortable seats that my father had designed. 'Cause he was six foot one and a half, and he designed a chair which was very comfortable, which was in fact marketed as the Prendergast chair.

Running the cinema was a full-time job, in which all the family were involved. The Prendergasts by this time owned cinemas in York, Malton, Pickering, Hull and Scarborough. June Lloyd-Jones played her part,

I was working in a theatre in Aylesbury so I came back to take over all the publicity, 'cause at that time we had seven cinemas altogether. We had stills, we had bill-posting, the whole thing was exciting. You looked in the glass cases on the outside of the cinema and made a pretty good judgement on what you fancied you'd go and see. We showed a highway film, and I have actually tramped the streets of York leading a figure on a horse, for publicity. There's none of that build-up now, you go cold into a cinema.

Mrs Prendergast as well as running the shop, took care of all the booking plans, working out prices for concerts, as her daughter explains,

As we were running a concert pretty well every weekend, that was very time consuming. She ran a home as well. Whatever job was needing to be done, we were involved in doing it. From selling tickets, to selling ice-creams, I used to work in the sweetshop.

In the 1950s, a host of young English singers appeared on the music scene, and the Rialto was one of their tour venues. They included such names as Tommy Steele, Marty Wilde, Cliff Richard and Adam Faith. June Lloyd-Jones met most of them,

Barry had a lot to do with Adam to start with, backed him on his early hits. Adam stayed with us. At that time they were just beginning to make their names, and they were all of an age with us. You didn't think of them as being stars, they were just somebody coming up to perform, and then they made their names after it. It was always enjoyable. There was an excitement in it, a spontaneity that seems to have gone now.

In 1956 when the York Empire closed down, Prendergast embarked on a policy of booking international artists, in conjunction with theatrical agent J W Collins, the father of actress Joan. Variety shows were to be staged weekly, aiming at family audiences.

One of the most famous acts to come to the Rialto was the Beatles. When the Beatles appeared in 1963, the most expensive seats were 12/6d. And it was while travelling from the Rialto to their next gig at Shrewsbury that they wrote the number one hit 'From Me to You'. Until then, 'Thank you Girl' was going to be the 'A' side of the record.

In 1961 the cinema was acquired by Mecca, after showing its last film, 'The World of Suzie Wong', and its magnificent £4,000 organ was sold for a mere £80 to a collector. The ballroom continued but in 1964, Mecca decided to build a dance hall on stilts behind the casino, in part of the car park. Eric Morley, assistant manager of Mecca in London, announced that this would be part of a £4 million expansion programme in the north. This did not materialise but in the late 1960s it became a nightclub, the Cat's Whiskers, which certainly flourished during the 1970s. It had another discotheque club, the Heartbeat, down the adjoining passageway. Mr Prendergast died in 1978, co-inciding with the end of another era.

In 1982 the police objected to the renewal of the music licence and the building changed again, from a nightclub to a snooker, pool, darts and leisure complex, run by the York Snooker and Leisure Centre. In 1985 the social club re-opened after improvements costing almost £400,000. The management planned to stage variety acts once again, but this did not happen and today the building is the Mecca Bingo Hall.

Inns of the Area: Lawson's Beerhouse and the Alma Tavern

William Lawson, a builder and publican of Alma Terrace was, by 1867, the proprietor of Lawson's Beerhouse. The business must have been quite successful because by 1885, Lawson owned numbers 1 to 10 of Alma Terrace, receiving between £10 and £12 p.a. rent for each one. Before his death in 1886, at the age of 74, he had also managed to build two houses in Ambrose Street and three in Frances Street. In addition to

Lawson's premises, there was a second hostelry by 1872, the Alma Tavern, run by John George Dawson at number 7.

In 1876 Isaac Oglesby became landlord, having previously managed the Britannia Inn in Walmgate. The Gazette of April 1874 was full of the story of his wife's elopement 'with two men and £600'. She had left Oglesby and seven of her eight children and fled to Sheffield. When the runaways were apprehended and brought to the York police station, a large crowd gathered.

'Yells, groans, hisses, and other tokens of disapprobation greeted their ears', reported the Gazette. The court case was dismissed despite the theft of Oglesby's umbrella and penknife. As his wife left the scene in a cab, she was heard to shout abuse at Oglesby, stating that she never wanted to see him again. A year later he divorced her, naming one of the men, Plews, a dancing teacher, as co-respondent.

By 1885, the Alma Tavern had closed down, and Lawson's Beerhouse was renamed the 'Sir Colin Campbell'. Sir Colin Campbell, Baron Clyde, had been a major general of British forces in the Crimea and is reported in the Dictionary of National Biography to have 'rendered the highest service at the battle of the Alma'. In fact, 'at the head of his brigade he landed in the Crimea, and he it was who really won the victory of the Alma'. In 1887 the establishment was taken over by Samuel Smith's Brewery, and soon after that became the Wellington Inn, which it remains today. The Duke of Wellington's regiment was twice stationed at the Infantry Barracks, playing a distinct part in Fulford life. The Inn consisted of three rooms, plus a billiard room upstairs which is no longer in use. In January 1897 new stables were built at the rear to house a cow! There have been many characters associated with the inn over the years, including a large ex-Cavalry man, Harry Hunter, who was landlord before World War I. George Kent remembers,

He used to amuse us kids. He'd stand on t'doorstep, then 'Fetch your stomach out Mr Hunter', [we would shout]. He could draw his breath and fetch it right up into his chest. He used to do it for us just to amuse us.

The inn has been adopted in recent years by the Campaign for Real Ale because of its almost totally original appearance, lack of pretensions, and the traditional hand-drawn beer pumps. In the last two years it has been added to the Statutory List by the Department of National Heritage.

Inns of the Area: Gotty's Inn

At the junction between the two fields facing the river beyond New Walk was Love Lane, a lane lined with crab apple trees, leading up from the river to an old inn, the New Walk Tavern (now called Lilac House). The inn sign was first noticed in 1872 according to George Benson's first survey of old inns in the city, but it must have existed before then, because William Kettlewell was licensee in 1870 at the age of 37, before moving to the Hudson's Arms Inn, Holgate Road. The house actually consists of three cottages made into one, two of which are pre-1850. The inn was sold again in 1875, and described in the Gazette as 'an undivided moiety of field and premises, including an arable field and beerhouse known as New Walk Tavern, and two cottages and strip of land'.

At the beginning of the century the proprietor was James Davison, who was succeeded in 1907 by forty-year old Albert Gott, son of George Gott, a farm labourer of Heslington Road. The establishment was thus always referred to as Gotty's up until 1936 when it closed down. It was rather a primitive place as far as decoration was concerned, all the furniture and fittings being wooden; and the Gotts kept a parrot which regularly patrolled the bar. Bare-fist fighting and cock-fighting were rumoured to take place in the area behind the pub. It was certainly a popular place, though. Mrs Florence Fenn remembers,

On a Sunday it used to be crowded because there was a lovely garden, with swings for the kiddies. You could sit out, there's a lot of land at the side of it.

And Mr Close recalls,

It was a real country inn, I think there was everything, bar sawdust on the floor. It had a garden with swings and two old trams with tops taken off and their insides used opposite the inn. You could sit outside with old benches and there was a table in the middle of it and further along there used to be a clay pit.

But in early 1911 Albert's wife Isabella (known as Polly) went missing one day, and when the police arrived, regulars reported that the couple had been in the habit of having strong, often violent arguments. Consequently the police dug up the garden, searching for the body; and although they found nothing, Mr Gott was still arrested on suspicion of murder. Several months later, a body was discovered by Alfred Key of Castle Mills Bridge; it proved to be Polly's and the verdict was suicide by drowning. She was buried on 15th May 1911, though the date of death was established as 20th January. Mrs Fenn, who cleaned there at the time, explains,

While I was working there, I was only fourteen, just left school. His wife was missing. He used to go off and leave me, when she was missing. I used to be nervous at that place. Well, the police came and they dug all the garden up. They thought he'd done 'er in. Anyway, they found her in the river. She had, she drowned herself.

Mr Close remembers another landlord, in the 1930s,

He worked on the trams so he had the job of cleaner with the depot. When we used to be going back to school many a time we saw him at the bottom near the Butter Stone. We'd cross the road because he used to pull us up and say, "Ere lad, just fetch me half an ounce of Battleaxe [tobacco]'. It was only a penny.

Or the landlady might also ask them to help out,

We used to have to get the barrels out for her. She'd give us half a glass of beer between three of us. I can still remember the old counter there and a little brass rail along the bottom where you stuck your foot.

Gotty's Inn, 1996

Inns of the Area: The Barrack Tavern

Almost opposite Briar House on Fulford Road lay the Barrack Tavern, which had been a public house since 1801. The first mention of it in local newspapers is an advertisement for its lease in the York Courant of December 1808. From the 1830s it was known as Hardcastle's Barrack Tavern, the landlord being John Hardcastle, who, in November 1853, was charged with condoning card-playing on his premises. Three soldiers of the 6th Inniskilling (now Enniskillen) Dragoons were guilty of playing cards there regularly, and their Colonel was, according to the Gazette, 'determined to have the case investigated, in order that the evil might be effectually put down'. Hardcastle pleaded ignorance and was exonerated, on the condition that he agreed to stamp out any recurrence of gambling.

Barrack Tavern, 1880s

In September 1880 the premises were bought by the Tadcaster Tower Brewery Co (later Bass North) and comprised not only stables, sheds for ten horses, loose boxes, outbuildings and an archway leading into a large yard, but also a cottage and baker's shop adjoining. The shop was Thomas Tittensor's, which later moved to the corner of Fishergate and Sandringham Street. Tittensor had come to York in the early 1850s, and in 1855 was a shopkeeper in Layerthorpe. By 1867 he had arrived in Fulford Road. Tittensor is not a common name and most of the Tittensors originate from the village of the same name in Staffordshire. Thomas was born in Newcastle under Lyme, only three miles away from the village. Tittensor was also the birthplace of Arthur Brittain, father of the author Vera Brittain, and the area had strong connections with the Wedgwood family of pottery fame.

Barrack Tavern, 1950s

By World War I, the shop beside the Barrack Tavern had become Timmy Todd's, selling cigarettes, sweets and ice-cream. Between the Inn and the Cavalry Barracks, the road was set back a little for a cab stand which was paved with setts in 1886. Major alterations were made to the Barrack Tavern in January 1966, and the name changed to the Fulford Arms on 17th May 1976, as a precaution against possible terrorist attacks at that time.

Inns of the Area: The Fishergate Inns

The Mason's Arms on Fishergate was built in 1838 and is known for its Gothic fireplace which originally came from the Castle gatehouse. It displays a variety of badges including the City Arms and White Rose of York. The pub was at one time called the 'Quiet Woman', and had a sign showing a decapitated woman with her head under her arm. The pub was offered for sale freehold in 1873, but was sold yet again in 1878. It included the basement, with its ale and spirit cellars, a dram shop with a plate glass window, tap room, large bar parlour, another parlour, a good-sized kitchen which was 'well closeted with Walker's Patent Kitchener', and two toilets. The first floor had a large sitting room, four bedrooms and three attics. Outside was stabling, with 'Walker's Patent Stable Fittings', and eight loose boxes. By 1902 this had increased to provide stabling for twelve horses - second only in size to the Seahorse Hotel on Fawcett Street, which could accommodate 25 horses outside and 25 travellers within, though in 1881 the Seahorse was advertising accommodation for 50 horses! The Mason's Arms also boasted three stalls, three capital saddle rooms, coach-house, piggeries, washing shed for horses, and out-offices. There were also 'commodious hay, straw and corn chambers', a well, soft water house and even a brewhouse. Beside the inn was a double cottage in the yard, two shops and dwelling houses, occupied by a tailor and a bootmaker.

This stretch of buildings, the inn and houses, was known as Union Place, Fishergate, in 1845. Quite a substantial place, covering 934 square yards! Another advantage was its right of wharfage on the River Foss behind the inn.

In 1883 tragedy struck when the landlord John Doughty lost his young wife, Elizabeth, who died at the age of 36. Three years later he married again, this time to another landlord's daughter, also called Elizabeth, daughter of Mintoft, landlord of the Bowling Green Inn, Lowther Street. A year later Doughty himself died, also at the age of 36.

Lighthorseman Bar, 1996

The Lighthorseman, on the corner of New Walk Terrace, is recorded in several books as being built in 1830 but did exist before that, probably in a slightly different place. There are records of a link with Waterloo. Troop

Sergeant Major Thomas Nicholson sustained a sabre wound during a charge in that great battle, was discharged from the army and in 1816 came to York and ran the Lighthorseman. He was still there on the 1841 census and died in September 1850, aged 60. His grave in York cemetery also includes three other people, one of whom is his son, who became a soldier like his father. The inn had stables, and sublet the yard to a cab proprietor in 1902. Today the pub retains its Victorian-style bar, with old lamp above depicting the Lighthorseman himself.

At the corner of Winterscale Street, on the site of the present St George's School, was the Fishergate Tavern, later the Brunswick Tavern, also called the Brunswick Hotel. This was then High Fishergate, the row of houses which separated Fishergate from Fulford Road. The inn first appears on record in 1872, and the landlord in 1891 was John Melrose Watherston, when it appeared in the directory as Watherston's Beerhouse. It was described in 1902 as having four bedrooms, an attic, a smoke-room, bar parlour, kitchen, cellar and serving bar. In 1919 Mrs Close was born there,

All the beer was drawn from the wood, they had to go down to the cellar for every pint of beer and draw it from the barrel. It was just a little pub, it had a bar and a snug. My grandmother actually had the licence and my mother and father lived with her because she was a widow.

The Brunswick had gone by the early thirties, and there are at least two other inns in the vicinity which no longer exist. The Soldier's Rest was situated on Fulford Road and was closed by 1897, and demolished between 1900 and 1905. At the bottom of New Walk Terrace, on the New Walk, stood the Pheasant Inn, until it was demolished in 1845.

The Edinburgh Arms on Fishergate was originally called the Edinbro' Castle Inn as early as 1839, and was then situated on the corner of Fishergate and Victoria Street (in the building now occupied by a butchers' shop). It was advertised for sale by auction in May 1857, complete with coachhouse, stables and yard, and it was described as being 'admirably suited for business purposes' and near to 'the new cattle market, the barracks, and the villages of Heslington and Fulford'. In 1874, a brewing house was proposed. In 1905 Frank Garner, the landlord, suddenly left for San Francisco but the licence was not transferred for another two years. In 1937 the inn was to be demolished in connection with the Fishergate improvement scheme, but this never happened. The name was changed again in 1976 from the Edinboro' Arms, to the Edinburgh, and the pub was completely refurbished in 1987. Today the sign once again reads Edinburgh Arms.

Beside the Edinburgh is a lane which was once the other end of Kent Street, and which leads onto Fawcett Street. The Woolpack Inn of 1845 has its entrance here.

Noel Attree lived at the Woolpack, where his family were tenants, in 1932,

My mother brought it up from a drover's pub to an up-to-date modern pub. The top room was beautifully appointed, with upholstered seats round. There was a middle room, called a tap room, and you went in another room further on, with a piano in. There was always somebody who could play the piano if they wanted. The Rialto was on the go with Mr Prendergast. He had some nice shows, and more often than not the people who were appearing would call in to the Woolpack.

Many stars who appeared at the Rialto in the 1960s period would frequent the Woolpack and the Edinburgh, and both Roy Orbison and Hank Marvin were spotted drinking in the Edinburgh before they became big names. More recently, since the arrival of the Barbican centre, the Kinks popped out in the interval of their concert there, to have a pint in the Woolpack, and a few months later Chuck Berry called into the Garden of India, next door, for a meal.

Fawcett Street is a street of inns. There are five in only a matter of yards - the Woolpack, Seahorse, Cattle Market (once owned by Samuel Smith's, now a restaurant), Edinburgh (strictly speaking this is on Fishergate) and the City Arms. These catered mainly for the cattle market population. The Cattle Market was also known as the Paragon Inn, and had a separate dram shop for out-sales. It was built in 1861.

In the latter part of the 19th century, there was another pub next door to the Woolpack. This was named the Glassmaker's Arms, due to its proximity to the glassworks. It was a rough-and-ready kind of place, which can be seen from the comments made by the licensing justices in 1902. They suggested that,

"the urinal should be partitioned off from view of the adjacent cottages".

This pub had also previously been called the Fat Ox, Glasshouse and Glassblower's Arms, according to T P Cooper. In 1885 the licensee John Dixon had his application for a music licence refused. The place was demolished in 1913, and the Gazette stated that it was referred to the Compensation Authorities. The Seahorse, on the other side of the Glassmaker's, was built in 1838. It was renamed the Shire Horses but has now reverted to its original name.

The City Arms is now a private sports and social club. At the turn of the century it had accommodation for 45 visitors, and stabling for their horses. The landlord was reputed to supply 'large dinners'. Mr Atkinson remembers it in the 1950s,

Farmers used to go a lot in there and have something to eat, a snack or something and a drink of beer, treat their mates and do a bargain on selling things. Maybe horses they wanted to sell, or a milk cow, they'd sell privately.

The cattle market and its clientele will be dealt with more thoroughly in our forthcoming book on Walmgate (to be published in December 1996).

12

Shops for Everything

Fishergate, Fulford Road, and many smaller streets off the main road were, from the very first, plentiful with shops. They played an important part in community life because they were friendly meeting places, where people went not so much to buy goods as for a gossip. Mrs D. recalls,

You didn't have to go into town to shop, it was as if you were in a town of your own, Fulford area. Better than any other area. Businesses were good, both Barracks were absolutely jam full.

Ken Richmond remembers seeing women going in just to talk,

I've been many a time sat here and watched people going in t'shop and come out about half an hour later, never buy owt, just go for a cal.

On Fishergate itself, are other interesting shops, including Alligator, the wholefood shop, Kooks Bistro, and within Sandringham Street is York Beer Shop, which provides all manner of unusual ales, wines and cheeses.

On the corner of Fishergate and Grange Street is Cooper's Corner, once Hattee's grocers, originally built as a baker's. It still has the old oven in the cellar, half bricked-in. John Smith's Brewery bought the premises to use as a beer-shop. The brewery began to sell off these old off-licences and in about 1985, Buckle's bought it, selling it to the present owners in 1990. In 1993, the shop began to incorporate a delicatessen offering a selection of exotic cheeses, fresh croissants, bagels, baguettes and ciabatta.

Cooper's Corner, Fishergate, 1934

But Mrs Josie Cooper believes that the days of the small friendly corner shop are numbered,

It's the same few people that support you. If every local householder spent only £3 a week, it would keep the corner shops open. 75,000 corner shops closed down last year, some that have been in families for generations. If I work it out, my hourly rate is 28 pence. I am lower paid now than I was ten years ago when I worked at Rowntrees. The government are taking in foreign companies like Netto, and this forces small firms out of business. Old people don't want to go and buy in bulk in the supermarket, here they can come and get one tomato, or one onion, or a small tin of beans. They can't there. They don't cater for single people, and all the big boys give all the perks to the big boys.

It is indeed a sign of the times that small businesses are being swallowed up by multi-national conglomerates, just as the river transport has gone in favour of lorries which pollute and congest our roads. It defies all logic.

Unfortunately another baker's, with an interesting history, is about to close down sometime in 1996.

Thomas Tittensor's bakery was originally situated next to the Barracks and later moved to the corner of Sandringham Street. Thomas died at 25 Sandringham Street in 1895. For many years a glass panel could still be seen in the front door. It bore the inscription - J. TITTENSOR. CONFECTIONER. Woolgroves' bakers took over the shop in 1928, and it remained there until the 1980s when the new owner removed the door, which is still in his possession.

Margaret Phillips in her memory of life in York in 1918 describes the magical experience of going out to Tittensor's on Good Friday morning for hot cross buns. She recounts a vision of 'lovely nut-brown loaves' which 'stood in fragrant rows all round' being arranged by a 'flushed Genie in a white hat, with a streak of flour decorating his forehead'. Thomas Tittensor is buried in York cemetery, and is commemorated by a cross near the beginning of the Butterfly Walk. His son, John, took over the business until his death in 1928.

Francis John Woolgrove originated from Banbury and founded his York bakery firm in 1908. He eventually had five shops, including what had been Tittensor's. The firm's group of shops closed in October 1993, and the baker's became Woodcocks. When this shop closes, it will truly be the end of an era.

In Alma Terrace in 1861 there were three small shops, one each owned by John Brown and John King, and the third at number 7 owned by Richard Jackson. William Bickerdike ran a grocery and ironmongers at number 3 in 1881. By 1900, the small shop at 45, next door to the Wellington, which had once belonged to William Lawson, had become a grocery, and 49 was occupied by a hairdresser. At 87 lived the baker, Francis Todd.

Co-operative Stores, Alma Terrace

The York Equitable Industrial Society's Jubilee History of 1909 mentioned that 'efforts are being made to carry out the wishes of the inhabitants of Fulford Road district, by securing suitable premises in that locality'. Later that year, the Society opened their Fulford branch (number 20) at 25 Alma Terrace, on the corner of Carey Street, and opposite the Police Station. A warehouse was built on the first floor, with a store and weighing room, and the second floor bedrooms became storerooms.

The photograph, below, shows the shop's car. Registered in May 1910, it was a 1300 hp coupe, of 10-12 horsepower, with green body and yellow wheels. It was a French car, made by Doriot Flandin et Pevent (DFP).

The "Co-op Car", Alma Terrace

By 1937 the shop had become the York Co-operative Society, and in the 1960s Doreen's corner store, until its closure in the mid-seventies. A few years later, it became a hairdressing salon, with a sunbed in the basement. On the left of the shop can still be seen the old winch, once used for hauling flour and provisions up to the granary.

In Ambrose Street Miss Hebden managed the general store at number 1 in 1885. In 1893 the owner Susan Meers went bankrupt as a result of 'sickness, bad trade, bad debts and fire'. The shop reputedly sold fishing tackle and monkeys at one time! In later years it was a second hand store, then a shoe shop, and in the 1980s a branch of the Fulford village bakery. In the 1880s Thomas Carbutt had the greengrocery at number 22, and Mrs Waller the off-licence at 45. On the opposite side were Atkinson's grocery and Hill's general store. By 1900 the street had been re-numbered, with odd numbers on the left hand side and even numbers on the right. There were general shops at 7 (Shaughnessy), 23 (Levi), 57, adjoining the laundry (Waud), 2 (Robert Oxberry) and 90 (Charles Walker). None of these shops remain now. No 9, Jacksons store, was the last to close in the early 1990s.

Frances Street abounded in shops for many years. In 1885 there were seven - Causebrook's butchers at number 1, Rymer's bakers at 26, Rushholme's general store at 41, Key's beer retailers at 65 (known to local children as the 'Black shop' because of the colour of its door), Jackson's greengrocery at 71, Dixon Potter's general store at 81 (built in 1888), and Smith's beer retailer and grocery on the corner. By 1900, the butcher and greengrocery had gone, number 11 had become Hodgson's general shop, Rushholme's was an off-licence owned by Braimes Breweries (until 1909 when the brewery went bankrupt and was taken over by John Smith's) and Smith's was renamed 'The Stores'.

Today this corner shop, known as Ben's, is the only survivor. Ben sells beer, sweets, cigarettes and a few groceries. But in 1900 the shop also sold glass, earthenware, china, hardware, brushes, iron and zinc as well as the usual provisions, and was also willing to do various repairs for customers.

In the early 1920s number 11 became a newsagency until 1967 when it changed into a wool shop and haberdashers, followed by a bakery. In early 1953 Mr Dawson the newsagent bricked up the passageway adjoining the house, which had been used as a shortcut through to the

Mrs Dawson and family,
Frances Street newsagents

Wellington, and had it altered to become part of his own living accommodation. He had, in fact, been paying rates for it for some time, and allowed it to be used by the public until it became abused. When the Mission Rooms at 29 transferred to its new abode in Alma Terrace, the 'holy window' was removed and the front room became a grocer's shop. The proprietor between the wars was known as Wiggy Wright, or in later years Daddy Wright, whose brother was renowned as a 'Professor Branestawm' character, an inventor of many things which went wrong, including a hair restorer. Wiggy was persuaded to act as guinea-pig, have his hair shaved off and apply the restorer. Not only was it ineffective but it completely destroyed the roots, rendering him permanently bald, as May Molloy describes,

He always used to have a lovely white coat on, but he always wore a straw hat, a boater, because he had no hair.

Ron Sheppeard also remembers him,

He was very good to everybody, lent money. People bought everything on credit. During the war he saved everything for the locals, like cigarettes.

The shop sold all the usual groceries, and some not so usual, such as gas mantles for a halfpenny each. Dixon Potter's 1888 shop at number 81 was occupied in the 1930s by Polly Potter, a very old lady who always wore a bonnet and sat in a room lit by candles. Number 42a had been a military laundry until 1933 when it became a greengrocers and wet fish shop until 1968. Mr Luxton, the greengrocer, went round the streets twice a week with his horse and cart (which he kept stabled behind the Barrack Tavern) selling fruit and fish. Ken Richmond recalls his visits,

He used to shout 'herrings'. You took your plate and he'd fill it for sixpence.

At number 4 lived Mrs Hemingway, the 'bookie's runner'. Locals took their bets on slips of paper, which were locked into a cloth bag just as the race began. Number 65 was an off-licence until 1977, and May Molloy remembers the owner,

Mrs Key at 65 was a very old lady. She sold bobbins of cotton and needles and she used to have the front of the window all full of different coloured cottons and

different sized needles. But still she was a greengrocer's and an ordinary grocer.

One regular feature of street life which is largely missing today was the horse and cart delivery. This included the milkman, who delivered milk, eggs and butter twice daily, the hot chestnut man, the herring man who appeared on Fridays, and the butter man with his pony and trap who allowed his customers to take a spoon out to the cart, and sample each of the many varieties. The rag and bone man was another character to be seen frequently, offering a balloon in exchange for any rags, as May Molloy found to her dismay,

Our kids used to take my things out of the drawer and give him them. 'I want a balloon.' Used to take towels and everything. Course he took them. I used to miss loads of things.

Number 41 was a general store and off-licence right up until the early 1970s and is now a private house. The last shopkeeper was a Mr Potts and local residents even wrote a song about him. Ken Richmond recalls earlier days,

You could go in and have a pint of beer in t'place, they'd just pull you a pint from t'wood, long as you drank it there.

Children could also earn a few coppers by running errands, as Ken recalls,

There used to be a woman up Frances Street and she always got called the 'penny woman'. We used to queue up on a Saturday morning 'cos first lad there used to go to t'Co-op which was just at top o' t'street for a weekly stamp. Used to get a penny for going, while t'rest of 'em'd get a lump of bread and jam.

At the bottom of Wenlock Terrace is a small passageway leading to Ordnance Lane, which was built as married quarters for the barracks in 1892. In this passage were stables which were originally occupied by the hunters owned by officers living in Wenlock Terrace. Mr Roy Luxton recalls,

The flat above the stables was originally the tackroom and storerooms. Then the tack room was the living room and the store rooms were bedrooms, the cooking was done on the landing and the laundry was done in one of the coach houses.

The stables and the flat were completely renovated in the early 1990s, to form new flats and lock-garages below.

Mr Luxton who owned the stables, which housed four horses, remembers that in the 1920s,

the flat over the stables was occupied by a family who ran a small business called Hillcrest Dairy. This consisted of a small box cart hand- pushed, with a milk churn inside and the measures on the outside. The stables were occupied by a coalman, who had two horses and carts, also a cobbler had one stable as a workshop.

At the top of Wenlock Terrace, facing the Cavalry Barracks, were four shops numbered 1 to 4 Wenlock Buildings. John Cross, who went into business in 1872 at the age of 28, as a grocer and provision merchant, rented part of the Buildings in 1885 from William Stott for £100 p.a., with a butchers, florists and drapers in the adjoining shops. By 1900 Cross owned it himself, and had expanded to open a post office. It would be another thirty three years before the Post Office would open on Fulford Road. Cross must have got a great deal of his trade from the Barracks, being in such close proximity. He later moved to live in Holly Lodge, beside Holly Croft (now 204-206 Fulford Road, a Grade II listed building), which was used during World War I by the Army Ordnance Corps, and for many years as a doctor's residence. Number 2 Wenlock Buildings was a butcher's, originally William Firth, and number 1 a fruiterer and florist - Thomas Bailey. By the 1920s the Post Office at number 3 had become Hutchison's drapers, and the fruiterer's a cobblers. The draper's grand-daughter, Mrs Peavey, remembers the shop vividly, as having sold not merely drapery items, but shoes, stockings, even cigarettes, and fancy garters which particularly amused the children because each was adorned with the face of a film star. Soldiers would come to the shop to order suits, and Mr Hutchison travelled to London to have them made up.

By 1936 Cross's grocery had expanded and stretched round the corner to encompass 1 Wenlock Terrace. John Cross also had grocers' shops in other parts of York, including Walmgate. Two years later, E J Nassau opened the Wenlock Bakery at 3 Wenlock Buildings, which proved enormously popular for its bread and cakes, and by 1951 it had been taken over by Mr H Grant, becoming known as both the Wenlock Cafe and Grant's dining-rooms, and being frequently patronised by the army as well as local clientele. In 1948 the rest of the block became part of William Jackson's Food Market (along with Cross's six other branches in York), and on 13th December 1965 the bakery and cafe were also incorporated into Jackson's Discount Supermarket, which by 1970 had become Grandways. In the 1980s it had reverted to the name Jacksons. The wine and spirits department, on the corner of Wenlock Terrace, was sold in 1994, becoming Adelle's hair salon (previously situated at number 1 Alma Terrace).

Further along Fulford Road, towards Alma Terrace, the two dwelling houses (now 196 and 198 Fulford Road) which were once part of Clarkson's land, became, in the later 1850s, Ivy Place. Next door was Ivy Cottage (not to be confused with Ivy Cottage on Fishergate mentioned in chapter 1) which Ambrose Walker rented to Rev William Cave of the United Methodist Free Church in 1885. Today these are a newsagent's, JD News, and Coopland's bakery/greengrocers. In 1907 Mr T Caffrey built a hairdressers and tobacconists shop on the corner of Alma Terrace, with an attractive glass door which had HAIRCUTTING AND SHAVING SALOON inscribed upon it. Mr Caffrey also built Derwent Cottage, at 1a Alma Terrace, as living accommodation. The shop was handed down to his son Arthur, a member of York Hairdressers' Federation for over 30 years, until his death in 1978 at the age of 72. His son Brian had taken over the business until he had to close the shop because of ill-health. Unfortunately he died in 1995. The shop is now a betting office called Fulford Bookmakers.

On Carey Street there are only two houses. The fish and chip shop on the corner of Frances Street once had a restaurant above it during the Second World War, the grandly-named Criterion Fried Fish Saloon. The other house is Stable Cottage, between the police station and the army stables which housed the barrack chimney-sweep above. This later became Smith's scrap-iron merchants, and then for many years Tebbutt's bookmakers (originally based at Derwent Cottage), a hive of activity on race days. For a short time, the premises had also, rather unbelievably, been occupied by a Special Branch of the army, who investigated military offences and liaised with the police station a few doors away.

Caffreys, 1930s

13

Two World Wars

In common with the rest of York, this area was affected considerably by the Great War, having a high record of casualties among those residents who fought for their country. George Kent from Alma Terrace recounts his own horrific experience,

I was up at Ypres when I got knocked out. When I got back from France I was in hospital in Birmingham from June to November before they discharged me. I joined up at Fulford Barracks. I took my youngest brother with me and they sent him home in my civilian clothes. They played steam because [another brother] had just got killed. He was only nineteen. We had a rough time of it. But people used to walk about giving you white feathers, as if you was dodging it. I was only in three months before I went to France. We had a rough time at Ypres, stood up to the thighs in water and I was only eighteen. They discharged me on full pension, in those days it was only £2 5s a week, and gave me six months to live. I was bald, I had all my hair burnt off with mustard gas. I've been grey ever since I was eighteen.

Another lady from the same street, Mrs Fenn, relates,

There was quite a lot killed, my husband was gassed. He was blind for so long and then he got his sight back, it was marvellous. He said, 'If there's another war, they won't get me!'

The Zeppelin which dropped a bomb on Low Moor behind the Barracks in September 1916 killed several horses and wounded at least one soldier. The top half of Alma Terrace was affected, for the Zeppelin left quite a bit of damage in its wake. Doors were blown off their hinges, and one house was covered in shrapnel which dropped through the skylight. Ken Richmond remembers his own father being permanently scarred by the experience of war, suffering a chest complaint 'through being gassed in the First World War'.

The photograph, opposite, is one of a set portraying York men killed in World War I, and includes several soldiers from this area. Private Kirkman of the Staffordshire Regiment was the son of Joseph Kirkman, a miller of 83 Frances Street, and Sapper S C Shaughnessy of the Royal Engineers was the son of Martin Shaughnessy, storekeeper and later butcher of 7 Ambrose Street.

After the war, more than one family was investigated by the government's Means Test. To qualify for aid, the family was only allowed to keep the absolute minimum of possessions such as a table, one chair per person, and a small amount of plates and cutlery. Sofas, easychairs, and a wireless were considered unnecessary luxuries and had to be sold.

This area was relatively untouched in the Second World War, at least as far as bombs were concerned. The bomb which fell on the cemetery on 10th August 1940 caused some damage, covering the gardens in Cemetery Road with pebbles and bits of gravestone. Winnie Richmond remembers walking by the river on a sunny Sunday afternoon in 1942, and meeting a friend and her baby,

I was telling her I'd got my bridesmaids' dresses with me, and she took my box to have a look at 'em and with that we could hear this machine coming. A plane was coming up that river, machine-gunning and nobody could believe it - he was machine-gunning and coming up towards Fulford and we all run. She ran with my box and I ran with her baby and I remember thinking 'Oh I must protect its head' and I put my hand over its head and we ran to Skeldergate Bridge. There were some air-raid shelters there and they weren't open and we all just hid under Skeldergate Bridge.

Fallen Heroes of York, First World War

Many of the houses in these streets had their own shelters in the back yard or garden. For those without them, there was a communal shelter at the Police Station and one on the green in the middle of Alma Grove. Those who lived nearby would go there, like Mrs Fenn,

We used to have a good laugh and all start singing 'Rose O'Day'. My husband used to be dogging out, looking if there was anything coming and I used to say, 'Come in 'ere, let's go together if we're going'.

Also on the green was an ARP post for the wardens of the area, next to a few allotments. The national motto was 'Dig for Victory' and the residents near the Grove obliged, and grew much of their food there. The ARP post, a small brick building, was manned by two volunteers every night, and had a telephone and bunk beds inside. There was also a pump for fire-watching. As well as the wardens themselves, each post had a boy messenger, who was left there when the sirens went. Mr Geoff Lee, later landlord of the Grapes Inn, was the messenger for the Alma Terrace area. He wore a navy beret and navy uniform with yellow epaulettes and 'messenger' written across the armband. The police station was at that time commandeered by the Army and gas masks were issued there.

In April 1942 during the Great York Air Raid, a bomb was dropped on the centre of Cavalry Barracks Square. One young soldier was killed and the horses caused pandemonium. The effect of the bomb made the windows shake and rattle in the surrounding streets. Mrs May Molloy in Frances Street remembers her windows shaking violently but not actually breaking because she had criss-crossed them with thick brown sticky paper as advised.

Mr Francis who went to Fishergate School and lived in Kilburn Road, remembers,

The raid on the barracks when the German aircraft machine-gunned the anti-aircraft gun pits, 'cos the following day most of us from our school went into the barracks looking for souvenirs. We found bullets which were embedded in the defence sandbags. As soon as we left school, it was on the cycle and to wherever there was a bomb fell or machine gun bullets. We used to go charging around looking for souvenirs - bomb fragments, bullets and parts of aircraft taken from where they crashed. We used to jump on the aircraft and break bits off. I got a piece of a German Messerschmitt ME 109. We had plenty of searchlights round the barracks, and at the latter end of the war, we even had rockets. We used to stand on the fence at the end of Kilburn Road and watch all the rockets going up when there was aircraft going over. And we got to a state when we could tell what particular type of aircraft it was.

At the Baedeker raid, we knew that this German fighter had come down and strafed the gunpits and killed several soldiers and that was as near as I wanted it to be to my house, which was roughly about between fifty and a hundred yards. They certainly did a lot of damage, a lot of roofs were shot up and it was in a pretty state next day.

My school had an Army Cadet Band, which, to my knowledge, has never been surpassed, at least in size. We had 21 bugles, 10 drums, three trumpets, used to go all over on church parades on a Sunday. I started on the cymbals, and went onto a bugle and finished up on a drum. The cadet old boys still meet in the Shire Horses in Fawcett Street [now the Seahorse].

Ken Richmond got married during the war, though the army weren't exactly co-operative,

I had to arrange through the army, to get married, six weeks before. And during those six weeks they sent us up to Scotland, we were doing a scheme called Dryshod and we were all over the place. The top half of Scotland was supposed to be the North Sea but nobody told us and we went down this road and the MPs stopped us and said, 'You're in t'middle of the North Sea'. We were all spread about all over t'place but our officers had all been sent back, they were supposed to have been killed in some action and they were back at camp. I was getting married on the Saturday and I was still there on the Friday so I got hold of an RAF officer. I told him I'd arranged it all, there were no letters, no post going out, so he signed me an old pass going to Glasgow somebody had in their pocket, and he initialled it. I got a lift on a motorbike from Old Cumnock to Cumnock station, I'd left all me kit, everything. Got to Carlisle, 'cos the enemy (us) in this exercise were wearing tin hats and the goodies were wearing forage caps, so it meant that I had a tin hat which was no fun travelling in, plus a tommy gun and all the ammunition. I gradually got to York and got arrested on York station, 'cos I'd shown my pass and he'd just initialled it at the bottom. When they have a used pass, they have to initial every word. They thought I was absent.

I got arrested but I gradually got to Win's house on the Friday. I was getting married on the Saturday but I didn't know what time so I had to go round there, 'I'm here, what time's wedding?' and her mam says, 'You can't see t'bride'. I was stood out in t'street but anyhow I got to know t'time. My pass was only for 2 days, so I spent one night in Scarborough.

At the end of the war, each street had a Victory party, as they had done in 1918. The street was hung with flags and bunting, with Union Flags everywhere. The children wore fancy dress and the adults sported their 'best' outfits. May Molloy was one of them,

We had one of those old gramophones, used to wind it up with a handle. His Master's Voice. We used to do the can-can, really funny.

The street would be full of trestle tables, covered with paper cloths and every household would contribute a home-made cake or other item of food. Banners were hung from one side of the street to the other at various intervals. War seemed to have the effect of uniting the community even further, although this sense of community spirit had existed from the beginning, as Ken Richmond observes,

It was a lot freer at the time. Most neighbours went into each other's houses for cups of tea and never worried about shutting doors. 'Cos you'd got nowt to pinch, no videos or owt like that. In fact when I left school you were proper high-class when you had a wireless. The wireless had an accumulator that had to be taken to Fishergate [probably to the Gem Radio and Battery Service at number 55] *to be re-charged. It cost sixpence. The tube went down into the floor, you poured water down every night, earth for the wireless.*

May Molloy agrees with these sentiments,

Everybody helped each other ... you never saw a locked door. In the summer we used to get all our work done and then we used to take our chairs outside in the front, at ten o'clock at night, because it was so warm. And somebody would put a gramophone on and we'd have a dance and we'd stop there. We had real good times.

Ken Richmond (right) in the army, 1943

14

The Riverside

New Walk had been a social meeting-place since the early 18th century when Georgian ladies and gentlemen paraded their fine costumes, the women displaying their pompadoured hairstyles, the men their powdered wigs and heavily rouged complexions. The walk was laid out and planted with trees in 1730, although Camidge's book of 1888, 'Ouse to Naburn Lock', states that a walk existed here as early as 1547. In 1739 the Walk was extended from the newly-erected Blue Bridge, originally a wooden drawbridge painted blue but since replaced several times, which was situated at the confluence of the Rivers Ouse and Foss.

Blue Bridge, c1905

The walk, being increased to one mile in length, was sheltered by a double row of lofty elms in 1740. Its name became the Long Walk, for obvious reasons, but then returned to the name of New Walk, which is a modified version of the much earlier name. CB Knight refers to the name Newark or Newe Werk being used in 1547. It must have been only a track at that time. In 1769 the bridge was replaced by a more attractive stone one, but that did not last long, as it was too low for vessels to pass under. In 1857 the third bridge (erected in 1801), another wooden one, began to disintegrate badly and was replaced by an iron bridge. This, the fourth bridge, was flanked by two cannons which had been captured as war booty at Sebastopol when it fell in 1855 during the Crimean War, and presented by the British government to York Corporation in recognition of the strong military links with the city.

About 800 such guns were taken from Russia, with other booty, and offered to many towns throughout England. Most guns were cast-iron like the York ones, but one or two were bronze. The bronze guns were used to make Victoria Crosses, and were kept at the Royal Mint until the last of the bronze was used in March 1942. The guns were mounted in 1858 with great ceremony on stone platforms, and remained there until they were sold for scrap metal in 1941, for the war effort. Each gun had a bronze plaque commemorating York men who 'fell during the Russian war'. Today's bridge, the fifth on the site, is from 1929.

In 1882, ornamental gates and railings were built near Blue Bridge, making New Walk more attractive. And, moving from the sublime to the ridiculous, the remains which can now be seen just within the gates are of public lavatories. Today the bridge is still regularly raised to let boats through to the Ouse from their moorings further down near Browney Dyke. If the river is in flood, the bridge may be left up. It is also occasionally used by firemen for practice training.

One boy from New Walk Terrace had an unpleasant experience there during the First World War,

I nearly lost my life when I was about seven or eight. I was walking along, coming home one Sunday afternoon, and the river had been in flood and I slipped in, by Blue Bridge. I could see people on the bank but nobody was making any attempt to get me. This soldier was coming over the bridge, on his way to the station to join his regiment and he dived in and pulled me out. He took me home and it turned out that he was the superintendent of some baths in the Manchester area. And I was the third person that he'd rescued and my father got him an award for it, his bravery.

St Andrew's Gilbertine Priory was founded in 1202 on this site, and given by Hugh Murdoc, the Archdeacon of Cleveland, to twelve Gilbertine Canons who built a house there, where it stood until the surrender of the monasteries in 1538. One historian relates how the monastery was opposite St Clement's nunnery and rumour had it that a subterranean passage ran between the two. But this fascinating piece of gossip is unfounded. Drake writing in 1736 calls this a 'ridiculous notion', as the nunnery was not in that vicinity.

Blue Bridge, 1920s

The only sign now of the Priory's existence is the fragment of stone wall at the bottom of Blue Bridge Lane. Since 1927 this has been the home of Shepherd Building Group, who moved there after a fire at their premises in Lead Mill Lane. In 1891, Freshfield Cottage was here, a pleasant house surrounded by trees. At the bottom of the lane is an ancient landing place where in 1847 a vessel landed with cargo of silk and tobacco which had escaped customs duty. Unfortunately the 'smugglers' were caught and one or two respectable and wealthy York families were disgraced by prison and financial ruin.

Pikeing Well, 1996

About halfway along the Walk, at the foot of the present Hartoft Street, is the Pikeing Well. John Carr the York architect, who became famous for the Assize Courts, Castlegate House and Bootham Asylum, designed a well house in imitation of a stone ruin, with Norman and possibly even Roman antiquities, to surround the natural spring located there. The land had been purchased from John Taylor, Lord of the Manor at

Fulford, in 1749, expressly to house an ornamental pikeing well. Two years later, Matthew Law was appointed Keeper of the Gate of the Well, and in 1756 the Well House was completed. The Fulford terrier of 1702 stated that the 'pikell' was rented by the Lord Mayor at a charge of £1 6s 6d. The Corporation should have paid Carr a fee of £88 13s for his work, but they deducted £25 from this because they had admitted him to the Freedom of the City in 1752.

The water from the Pikeing well was used for both drinking and medicinal purposes. It was considered to be of immense value in the treatment of sore eyes. A keeper opened the door regularly for citizens to have access to the water. Later, the well became part of the Fulford Grange estate, but it was eventually released to the citizens of York. The well continued to be used until the Ministry of Health decided that it was unfit for drinking and should be closed and the water supply was cut off in November 1929. Apparently, the 'pure' water had ceased to be true to its name, because water drained from the York Cemetery was found to be coming up through the well! The well-house remains and has been renovated in the last decade, becoming a Grade II listed building.

A letter was received by the York Chronicle in April 1816, which ranked the trees in New Walk as equal in beauty to the Minster. When the news leaked that forty-one elms were to be felled, the public protested heavily. However, despite protests, trees have continued to suffer this fate spasmodically. When a poplar tree was felled in February 1888 at the southern end of New Walk, so that the War Department could construct a wharf with craneage power to land military stores for the Ordnance depot, the Council sold it for 30s. In 1889, new trees were planted, and these are probably now the oldest surviving trees on the Walk. The Walk was also improved by the addition of new gates and palisades, and a number of seats along the riverside. Tramlines were dug into the middle of the walk, to enable equipment to be transported up to the Ordnance Sub-Depot, through the now blocked-up entrance. The Depot stood on what is now Hospital Fields Industrial Estate, and was closed in 1957.

New Walk, 1900s

After a campaign in the late 1980s by a local resident, the council filled in the lines which were becoming increasingly quite dangerous. Ken Richmond remembers the depot,

The Ordnance factory was where they stored a lot of bombs and shells. Oh guns, not shells. They had a range down there, a firing range, and they used to test them there. I think it was for small arms. There was the military hospital there, and that used to take all t'overflow from t'County. They used to search everybody coming out of there. A pal of mine worked there and he used to get picked on that many times to be searched, in t'finish he used to just walk straight in and hold his hands up! He did that a few times and they never bothered him after that.

During 1995-6, the old wall has been cut through and a new pathway has appeared leading from the end of New Walk, through into Hospital Fields estate.

In September 1921 a programme of thinning and lopping the trees in the Walk cost the Council £350 to carry out. It was adopted as a scheme by the city's new Unemployment Committee, although it only actually provided work for three men. Probably the biggest operation amongst trees was in September 1980 when the Council sadly chopped down a vast number found to be suffering from Dutch Elm disease, replacing each destroyed tree with an infant sapling.

At the southern end of New Walk, the land as far as Fulford Ings was divided into three fields, rather unimaginatively christened the First, Second and Third Fields, although the Third Field was also referred to as the Hilly Field. Adjoining the Second Field was 'Tar Kelly's Field', named after a very early ferryman of whom nothing is now remembered except the name. In the centre of this was a large pond surrounded by bulrushes and elderberry bushes, a good resource for many local wine-makers. The whole field was always marshy and the home of many waterhens. In winter the pond froze and in the 1920s and 1930s young people would spend hours there. Winnie Richmond reminisces,

We hadn't skates, used to slide about just in our shoes. We thought we were skating. We used to get a candle and stick it in a jam jar. We put candles round the edges to light the pond, we made our own enjoyment.

At the edge of the fields there still exists the path called Love Lane, also known as Lover's Lane for obvious reasons, and Dirty Dick's Lane because it was reputedly haunted by an old tramp. Cows grazed on most of the third field except the lower, flatter part which was the venue of football matches for both Fulford Corinthians and the Weltonians, the team from the Wellington Inn, whose white shirts and blue tops were easily recognised by local spectators. The team played many friendlies in villages around York, including what was then RAF Heslington, as well as arranging frequent outings and trips for the members and their female guests.

The first and second fields frequently saw scores of Fulford people strolling out, especially on Sunday evenings. The riverside was always considered by people in the locality as the chief source of entertainment. During World War II, throughout the country, people arranged 'Holidays at Home Week' because no-one was able to travel. The New Walk was adopted for such a week, and sectioned off for swimming and diving races, with a band entertaining the 'holidaymakers' and plenty of refreshments. Strangely enough, this was the site of the Sheep Wash, marked on the Ordnance Survey map of 1849!

Mr Ray Close played in this area,

There was Cooping Close at the bottom of Fulford Cross, which was a big house with an orchard, an apple orchard grown for wine. They were wine merchants. We used to have a plank, we got it out of the river, and nine of us used to hang on the end. We used to get little John and stand him on the plank on their fence and we used to walk to the other side and fill these two bags with apples. They had about eight Black Aberdeen terriers, they used to be barking and carrying on. And up Fulford Cross there was some walnut trees, they cut them down when they started building the new school and we used to get these trees for walnuts. When you went to school you daren't show your hands - all brown.

In later years Mr Close would go onto the first field to spend the night,

We used to spend hours down there, and we had a tent made out of a big sack canvas. We'd sleep underneath that palace on the river bank.

York swimmers were encouraged to make the most of the facilities available, and in 1943 the Corporation set up a diving stage, from the concrete landing stage at the end of New Walk, with several dressing cubicles within an enclosure. Mrs Gibson of New Walk Terrace had been one of the pioneers of the scheme, which was designed to allow expert swimmers to spend more time in the water. Beginners were discouraged, however, as the river was too deep, at least seven foot in places. To deal with any accidents, the Corporation appealed for voluntary life-guards to be in attendance and a patrol boat in position.

Every year on November 5th, the first field was chosen as the location for an enormous bonfire, for all the children (and many adults) in the vicinity. There were few fireworks, being too expensive an item, but everyone still enjoyed the occasion. After the Second World War, the first and second fields were transformed into the Fulford Tip. Originally the fields were much lower than they are today, but the allotments which bordered on Love Lane were liable to flood. The Council had planned to build a swimming bath there in 1899, but this was abandoned.

They still considered the possibility of building on the land but the ground had to be covered with spoil to a height of more than ten feet, then left for ten years to settle. In the mid-seventies it was levelled off, and a thin layer of soil covered the rubbish which, like compost, was turned back into soil. Children would climb up the mound to play 'I'm the King of the Castle'.

In 1958 the tip was considered as a potential sports ground, then in 1960 the Council announced that it was to be changed from a Public Open Space to an Industrial Area. In July 1961 the Streets and Buildings Committee authorised that Love Lane should be raised to the level of Maple Grove, a post-war development which stretched from Fulford Road, opposite the Infantry Barracks, to the riverside. Once the level was raised, Love Lane changed from a narrow avenue with trees at either side, to a mere track adjoining the field. The first field, which once boasted infinite varieties of wild flowers, such as harebells and milkmaids, and scores of mushrooms which would be faithfully gathered each morning at dawn, is now only grass, covered in summer with clumps of horse-radish, and here and there a few toadstool rings. The two goats from Lilac House (the old New Walk Tavern) grazed for many years on this field. Down towards the river there had been a private boatyard, where boats were taken for repair, keeling and overhauling. Although the land is railed off, it is now sadly overgrown with weeds and nettles. Beyond the boatyard, the land suddenly plummets again, as it approaches Fulford pumping station. The river edge at this point is lined with willow trees, from which local children once made bows out of strong bendable branches, and transformed straight shoots into arrows. One such child was Ken Richmond,

If you weren't at school together you were up fields making bows and arrows. You made your own amusement. We used to go down on t'fields, where it's green, there was three fields and we used to go in them. And swim in the river, that was the main thing.

When the council proposed a touring caravan site for the first field in 1979, many petitions and a stormy public meeting convinced them that everyone in the area was totally opposed to the suggestion so the idea was abandoned, and fortunately the land remains open.

Some people spent all their spare time by the river, deeming it a far healthier occupation than sitting by the fireside at home. After all it is less than five minutes walk from Ambrose Street until one is 'in the country'.

For many years, a houseboat named the Yvette was moored at the Ordnance Jetty, New Walk. The boat originally had two Rolls-Royce Merlin engines but they had been taken out. The family who owned this ex-naval motor yacht fenced off part of the grass at the riverside for their own garden, and the War Department's annual rent of 2s 6d for the jetty was transferred to them. Eventually though, in December 1959, the council told the owners to remove the boat.

The Ferry

According to the Daily Express of 23rd October 1963, in which an article on the New Walk Ferry appeared, 'the ferry is described in historical documents of hundreds of years old'.

In 1849 Joseph Gilliam, who had leased the Skeldergate crane house and ferry together with New Walk Ferry, died, and his widow Mary applied to take over the lease. Despite several other tenders the Council agreed to let the rights to her in March 1850 by ticket for three years, at an annual rental of £90. The Gilliam family had leased the crane and ferries since 1797. In 1869 the lease was taken over by a man named Dawson, possibly the same Dawson who managed the Alma Tavern.

The next recorded ferryman is Patrick Flanagan, who was granted the privilege of running the New Walk ferry for one year, by the Ouse and Foss Navigation Board in 1919, at an annual rental of only £31. The ferry crossed the Ouse from the foot of Ambrose Street to Rowntrees Park. Tolls had to be subject to the Committee's approval, and nothing was to be placed on either bank or in the river. In 1928 'Matty' Myers became ferryman. Apparently his biggest job was teaching the local boys to swim.

Ken Richmond was one of them,

Many a time he'd rake us out o't'water and say, 'I'll learn you to swim'. I used to have awful habit of walking in t'water, falling in. He used to put a rope out at back of his ferry boat and put it round us and tow you across and that's how I learnt to swim. He taught loads of kids. He had a little hut with a stove in, all t'kids used to gather there and he used to tell us tales. If you were one of his pals, he used to let you scull it over a bit, but I could never get hang of it myself. He made most of his money off girls going to Terry's. Take your bike across, it was tuppence ha'penny and then he'd charge extra for your bike.

The boys dived off the wharf at the end of New Walk, and used this and the crane as part of their play area. Mrs Close remembers when the ferry fare was a penny,

When I was young I used to swim across the river with a penny in my bathing cap, in case I couldn't swim back.

Following Matty Myers came a succession of people for short periods, including Mr Fairbairn, a farmer from Bishopthorpe, Mr Bristow, Mr Smith the taxi-cab proprietor from Alma Terrace, Mr Broadhead and Mr Ron Sheppeard. The ferry was occasionally used for trips downriver on summer evenings, and Ron Sheppeard certainly enjoyed that,

We used to get some crates from the Wellington. I used to sing a bit and we used to go serenading down the river. The bank on a Sunday morning was full of anglers and they used to run a little sweepstake among themselves, there'd maybe be forty or fifty anglers on one side. On a night we used to go eeling, we used to get some crates and we'd throw our rods in and then just sit and catch eels. We never used to catch many but we'd sit all night and have some great times.

The ferry was started up again in 1952 by the newsagent from 11 Frances Street, Mr Len Dawson. The business was a successful one because there was plenty of contract work from the Ordnance Depot and workers travelled across the river daily to Terry's factory in Clementhorpe. When the factory moved it was still quicker than going by road. Soldiers billeted in Dringhouses used the ferry and then walked the rest of the way. But race days were always the most popular. Mr Dawson utilised two boats, one of which was powered by an Austin Seven engine,

I could get twenty in my ferry. When the races were on, we used to charge threepence, it went up from tuppence, and we made £500 that first summer I took that ferry. Saturdays and Sundays we were going all the time, backwards and

forwards, backwards and forwards. I used to get young lads to come and help me. During the week you used to get workers coming across.

At the bottom of Ambrose Street steps, a path was worn through the grass down to the river, then a second set of steps led to the bank itself. This was where the ferry had its base, with two poles fixed in the water and a painted sign over the top which read FULFORD FERRY. There was also a hut of creosoted wood where the oars could be locked in over night. However a teenage boy who temporarily helped out had other ideas for its use.

One of the householders of Holly Terrace had seen several boys enter the hut, and, growing suspicious that it was being used as an illicit gambling den, she telephoned the police who arrived to search it. The boys were discovered to be playing cards, a harmless occupation to pass the time when the ferry was not operating. This did not happen very often because the ferry ran in all weathers. Obviously, summer was by far its most hectic time when, apart from the regulars, families often wished to cross to the Park or the swimming baths. But trade continued in the winter, come rain or snow, usually just three times a day - early morning, lunchtime and teatime. There were only two things which prevented the ferry from venturing out. One was when the river flooded. At this time the boat could be seen in the distance still attached to the chain below the river wall, though the hut had disappeared completely under water. (Fortunately the houses in this area are not heavily affected by floods. Even in the great floods of 1947 and 1982 the water only reached the top of Ambrose Street steps). The second hindrance was during a heavy storm. Mr Dawson relates,

If there was an electric storm you never went across. I've sat in that hut and seen lightning run down the river, just like a snake, banging and cracking.

When Len Dawson began to operate the ferry, he was told by an ex-Sergeant Major from the Ordnance Depot that an earlier ferry, used specifically by the Depot, had merely been a round tub with a scull at the back and seats all round, which had sunk during the First World War. The ferry has never sunk since then, although passengers have occasionally fallen into the water! One man, who enthusiastically offered to help a woman with a large coach-built pram to get in, pushed the boat out without realising it. He had one foot on the bank and one in the boat, and 'he did the splits and ended in the water. He got the pram in and then just disappeared'. As well as providing a service for people on both sides of the river, the ferry was also instrumental in saving lives of children who had fallen in.

During the Tattoo of 1955, the boat ran to and fro almost continuously. It would return with spectators each night, sometimes as late as 2 am, by the light of a single lantern. When Mr Dawson left the area in 1957, Mr Ernest Driffield who had become his partner took over full ownership. In 1964, the Council agreed to pay £70 for the construction of a landing stage on the Clementhorpe bank of the river. Mr Driffield ran the ferry until 1967, with the help of his daughter, Pauline, and four sons, John, Kevin, Christopher and Howard. An article of October 1963 named the three younger sons as 'Britain's youngest ferry crew', their ages being fifteen, eight and five.

Kevin, the fifteen year old, taught his younger brothers to scull the twelve foot long boat, and when his father and elder brother were at work, he would take charge of the ferrying, charging his customers fourpence a head. But the Yorkshire Evening Press of 15th March 1967 carried the notice 'For sale, eight passenger scull'. Mr Driffield no longer had the time to operate it as often as he would like, because of his demanding job. His family were growing up and working themselves. Trade had gradually slackened too, with the departure of troops from the city, and vandals had damaged the boats more than once. Each time they were smashed, it meant that they had to be towed up to the lock basin for repair.

In March 1982 Jim and Sally McGurn briefly started the service up again as "Rowntree Park Community Ferry", with a rowing boat which was run only on Sundays and special occasions such as race days and the Pope's visit to the Knavesmire in May of that year. But the venture did not last long, due to the heavy costs involved, although it carried over three thousand people during its brief life.

On Sunday 14th July 1996, the new City of York Council, organised a ferry service for one day, to take people over to Rowntrees Park for the Park's 75th birthday celebrations. The three 8-seater boats came from Easy Rider Leisuredeck, run by Tetley's Brewery Wharf, and operated throughout the day on both sides of the river. The New Walk site was at the end of Farndale Street, further along from the original ferry site. The cost to travel over was only 35p, and the experience of crossing the water on such a day, with the sun dancing on the surface, was very pleasant. The Green Party engaged the company again for the August Peace Festival, replacing the small inflatable dinghy used for the festival in 1995.

Now that there is no longer a ferry at New Walk, the residents definitely miss the service, especially as it takes nearly an hour to walk round, whereas the ferry ride lasted less than five minutes. Those who regularly patronised the ferry still feel a sense of loss at its demise. After all, as one local person put it, 'The ferry was a part of Fulford existence'.

15

The End of an Era

New Housing

Within Alma Terrace, adjoining the wall of Briar House, was an oblong piece of land fringed by trees, Alma Gardens. In July 1911 the Council's Streets and Buildings Committee bought the gardens, which measure 1444 square yards, from Emily Pearson for the sum of £1,300. In the Gazette of 18th November 1911, this was described as the 'City Council's first scheme to house the working classes'.

The Council's idea was to build thirty cottages to house the displaced families who were rendered homeless by the demolition of houses in Pavement, when Piccadilly was built. The land was to be laid out so that the houses faced into a rectangle 214 yards long and 46 yards wide, with trees planted round the edge. The houses were to be built in six blocks of four and three blocks of two. Each one would have three bedrooms, a living room, scullery, pantry, coalhouse, wc, and bath in each scullery with hot water, and the rent was to be 5s a week. In the centre of the grove it was hoped that a bowling green could be provided. The whole scheme was very significant because the houses were the first Council houses in the city, in line with national schemes set up after the Housing of the Working Classes Act 1890, 1903 and 1909.

The scheme went into operation in October 1912, after the site had been cleared of all existing buildings and trees. The work was contracted to Gilbert and Lawrence Lough of Blyth, to the design of F W Spurr, City

Architect. The Loughs had also built the Mission Rooms in Alma Terrace in 1900 and would erect Knavesmire School in 1914. They took a temporary office in Coney Street and completed the work in 1913, at a cost of £6,398 0s 9d. In 1923 the Housing Committee agreed to sell the houses and over the next few years twelve were sold privately, a process which has continued.

In 1972 the City Council named Alma Grove as a general improvement area. In their 'New Homes for Old' plan, Leeman Road and Alma Grove were the two main areas eligible for 75 per cent modernisation grants, which aimed to tackle the problems of housing and the environment. The central island in the Grove was developed in 1975 to provide a layby for six cars, a paved area for pedestrians and a grassed section including trees. A few yards from Alma Grove was a side lane (almost opposite Carey Street) which was once the site of Swann's Farmhouse, or Fern House. Edward Beilby Swann lived there from the 1880s to his death in 1922, selling eggs, milk and butter to local families. Apparently Edward's daughter Lucy Swann took the cow for a walk down the Terrace each evening. The Swanns delivered milk in the area, as George Kent remembers,

They used to come round carrying a can, knock at the door and you took a basin, and they had a kind of scoop with a measure and they used to put it in. Tuppence a pint.

In 1893 a stable was also built for the horse belonging to the police station. The land later housed fourteen lock-up garages. The two cottages which formed numbers 28 and 30 Alma Terrace are now razed to the ground, along with the cow sheds.

In January 1991, work was started on building Alma Court, a new group of houses, off Alma Terrace, on the land which had been Swann's. These houses have their own gardens, and carports.

As early as the 1930s, the area was beginning to change physically. In March 1938 a clearance order was issued for the seven houses which comprised Staveley's Buildings in Alma Terrace, together with numbers 76 to 82 of the Terrace. After they were demolished, being 'unfit for human habitation', Mr Johnson, the coal merchant, had a garage built on the land to house his lorries. In the early 1960s, Rington's Tea Merchants opened a depot on the spot. Staveley's Buildings, owned in 1885 by Maria Staveley, had once housed York's reputedly largest family, the Thorpes, who were featured on the BBC Radio programme 'Down Your Way'. By the middle of the century, families were becoming smaller. In the 1920s, one fairly typical property in Frances Street housed two adults and eleven children. Ken Richmond, a friend of one of the sons at the time, recalls,

I used to come from our house to call for him to go to school. His mother always had this great big jug of cocoa on t'hob. When you got in, first thing you got was this red-hot cup of cocoa. It was as thick as pudding. I don't know where she put them all, I think they must have slept in relays.

It is also a fact that whereas now families move in and out of the area fairly frequently, the trend was once for families to move from one house to another within the area, an easier process then because houses were rented. Mrs Fenn, for example, lived in Ambrose Street for ten years, in Frances Street for twenty years, and Alma Terrace for nearly fifty years.

In 1950 the Hen Run disappeared. The City Architect, Charles Minter, gave planning permission on 11th April, and four council flats and four maisonettes were built, becoming numbers 13 to 20 Holly Terrace. The erection of the flats encouraged the residents to step up pressure on the council to have the Terrace re-numbered. Yet it was not until 1967, after the urging of the City Engineer, that the council relented. Numbers 1 to 8 (known as 'Big Holly Terrace' because of their extra storey) had been built first, and numbers 9 to 12 ('Little Holly Terrace') added later.

A New Era: the 1970s and 1980s

As part of its development programme, to provide accommodation for families in need, the Catholic Housing Aid Society, part of the Family Housing Association, acquired one house in Frances Street and three flats in Wenlock Terrace. The former was badly in need of modernisation and improvement and so its acquisition served the community by rehabilitating the property, and at the same time provided a low-cost rented home for those who needed it. In 1972 when many British Asians were ejected from Uganda and settled in England, the Society offered this house. A report on the re-housing of Ugandan Asians, 'Green for Come', stated that,

"Originally the Catholic Housing Aid Society offered one large house to ten people - father, mother, widowed sister, three daughters and four sons."

The family were a welcome addition to the community during their stay there, though there were instances of prejudice, including anonymous letters. One of the daughters told me that, whereas she had been a teacher back in her own country, she would have to start from scratch here and train again if she wanted to teach. The only job she could get was factory work.

On 7th June 1977 the streets re-created their earlier VE Day and Coronation parties by celebrating the Queen's Silver Jubilee in their accustomed way. The Frances Street party began at 2pm with games, dancing, fancy dress children's parade, adult races, tug of war, tea and communal singing. Ted Tebbutt, the bookmaker from Carey Street, opened the proceedings. In the evening the Street Ball took place, music blared forth, and the residents ate and drank, talked and danced the night away. For older residents, this evoked memories of all the other parties held in the street, a phenomenon which has largely disappeared in the 1990s.

Silver Jubilee Party, Frances Street, 1977

Ron Sheppeard talks of how the community spirit,

seemed to die in the 1950s. Before that you could leave the doors open all night. People used to sit on their doorsteps at 12 or 1 o'clock at night talking. That wasn't just one little group, that was the whole street. It was a marvellous place to live, a marvellous spirit there.

May Molloy of Frances Street agrees, adding that,

It is a good street this ... there is still that spirit.

In 1981, Holly Croft was released by the army, who had owned it since 1903, and taken over by the Social Services Department, from Ryedale House in Piccadilly. The front room with its large bay windows and high ceilings made an ideal meeting-place for a lively old people's group on

Mondays and Thursdays, playing an important part in the lives of local pensioners. In 1987, the ladies of the Thursday Group began to knit for children in Ethiopia and Mozambique. Mrs Flo Fenn had only learned to knit two years previously, being taught by Sister Magdalen of the Sisters of Charity of St Vincent de Paul. After an appeal from 'Save the Children', groups all over York produced sackfuls of tiny woollen jumpers, and Flo Fenn knitted hundreds.

The Royal Signals Association Club, located in the grounds of Holly Croft, once the scene of social get-togethers, wedding receptions and whist drives, has long since closed down. Part of the original grounds have now become a doctor's surgery and health centre. In 1982 some of the outbuildings of Holly Croft were renovated ready for use by St Dymphna's Playgroup for mentally handicapped children, who had moved from their unsatisfactory premises at the Grange after floods ruined the room they had been using.

Unfortunately the building began to crumble and in October 1993 a surveyor pronounced it unfit for use. The day centre was described in this way, 'it sways in high winds, the steel in its concrete frame is corroded and the brickwork is unstable. Half the shell is asbestos and one end is locked up, too dangerous to enter'. After the Yorkshire Evening Press highlighted its plight, many people called to pledge support, either financial or practical. Fund raising events were held and money came in. Community action project workers stepped in and undertook the challenge to build new premises for York's only special-needs nursery. Within eighteen months, a new premises opened up in Hamilton Drive, Acomb.

The houses in Wenlock Terrace, once the home of the professional classes, have become sadly dilapidated in parts. There are three guesthouses, the well-established Fulford Road Working Men's Club, and the rest of the buildings are flats.

In 1980 Mrs Agnes Wilde, the oldest verifiable centenarian in York (according to David Poole's research), died at the age of 108, and is buried in York Cemetery. She had been born Agnes Saynor in Huntingdon, Cambridge, in January 1872 and lived at 67 Frances Street in her early years from 1889 to probably 1906, with her father (a groom/coachman), mother, and six siblings. At least one other centenarian lived for a time in this district. George Gledhill, who was born in 1894 in Wharfedale, lived in Alma Terrace for over forty years from 1952 to 1994, before leaving the area.

Another person whose family had lived in Frances Street, was Bob Littlewood, Superintendent of Works at York Minster. He was the man who led the team of craftsmen who carried out the four-year restoration following the Minster fire in 1984, and consequently was awarded the OBE and received the freedom of the Worshipful Company of Carpenters in recognition of his work. His family had served the Minster for several generations and one neighbour in Frances Street remembers his grandfather coming home from work always wearing his white apron and cap.

Some traditions never die, and the Fulford Show is one example. It takes place annually on August Bank Holiday Monday, the archetypal village show, where those who live in the parish (Naburn to New Walk Terrace) are encouraged to exhibit their home-grown tomatoes, marrows and cacti, their tapestry and knitted toys, their photography, jams and marmalades, wines and beers. The children bring their miniature gardens, models of Wallace and Gromit, decorated eggs and hedgehogs made from root vegetables, and come away thrilled with First, Second or Third Prize certificates.

16

Into the 21st Century

During the 1990s, a number of improvement schemes have revitalised both New Walk and the streets off Fulford Road. These include new street lighting, road surfacing, more litter bins and rubbish skips, new benches and trees planted, and other rebuilding work. The introduction of neighbourhood forums which meet regularly at St George's School in Fishergate, and are funded by the council, give residents their own say in how the funds are used, making choices about renovations and improvements in the area.

A few years ago, Margaret Bracegirdle and a few friends, who were interested in matters concerning the local area, formed the 'New Walkers'. The group have met once a year to stroll the length of the New Walk and donate a fee to the Macmillan Nurses charity for the privilege.

Plans are now being made for a bridge to be built across the river, a crossing of forty metres, from the end of New Walk to Clementhorpe, close to Rowntrees Park. The 'Millennium Bridge' should be in place by the year 2000. The bridge will serve pedestrians, cyclists and wheelchairs. This year (1996), the new City of York Council are applying to the National Lottery for funds. In March, a competition was launched to design this bridge, and the group of residents behind the scheme formed themselves into York Millennium Bridge Forum.

Perhaps the biggest scheme in recent years, has been the development of a cycle track which stretches from Ouse Bridge in the town to Blue Bridge, and then along New Walk across the fields up to Hospital Fields

New Walkers, 1995

Estate. The cost of this (£27,000 to join the latter part of the route) has been part funded by Shepherd Building Group, since the building of their new premises on the corner of Hospital Fields Road. Sir Donald Shepherd was shown in the local press as leading the way, cycling from his home in Dringhouses along the track to work each day, and thus avoiding most of the traffic, particularly on the A19. He emphasised the safety aspect of using this track and this has encouraged far more people to cycle to work, with the path being divided by white lines in the centre, which separate cyclists from pedestrians.

So time is moving on, too quickly in most people's opinion. Life does not stand still. It is important that we hold onto our heritage, that we preserve documents and artefacts for use by future historians. It is also crucial that we pass on orally, down through the generations, the reality of how we lived. It is this combination of oral and written history which can allow us to build up a picture of 'how it really was'.

New Walk Cycle Track, 1996

About the author ...

Van Wilson is a graduate in English and American Studies, and wrote her thesis on the subject of 'Madness in 20th Century Women's Literature'. She has been involved with oral and local history for several years, and has had articles published in several magazines.

Before starting to write books, she spent eight years in bookselling and gained the Diploma in Bookselling with distinction in five subjects.

She is the author of 'The History of A Community : Fulford Road District' (1984), 'Alexina : A Woman in Wartime York' (1995) and 'Rich in all but Money : Life in Hungate 1900-1938' (1996).

Van works as administrator for a young people's theatre company, and is married with two children.

About the photographer ...

Simon I Hill gained Diplomas in Photography and Art & Design from Blackpool College of Art in 1985, and an MA in Film and Television from the London Institute in 1992. He was elected a Fellow of the Royal Society of Arts in 1989, and of the Royal Photographic Society in 1991.

He has had photographs published in many national and international journals and periodicals including *The Sunday Times Magazine, National Geographic Magazine, The Illustrated London News* and *Der Spiegel.*

As a photographer and chartered designer, Simon is Proprietor and Creative Director of Scirebröc - a design group which he founded in 1983. Simon is married with two children.

About the ARC ...

The ARC - Archaeological Resource Centre - is an award-winning hands-on exploration of archaeology for visitors of all ages, designed by the York Archaeological Trust to complement its Jorvik Viking Centre in Coppergate. Located in the beautifully restored medieval church of St Saviour, close to the Shambles, the ARC has an ever-changing programme of special exhibitions, children's activity mornings, lectures, videos and other events throughout the year.

For further information, telephone 01 904 654 324.

The ARC is open all year, including weekends and evenings for pre-booked parties of more than 10 persons. To make a party booking for the ARC or the Jorvik Viking Centre, telephone 01 904 613 711.

Open to the public:	Monday to Friday	10am to 5pm
	Saturday and Sunday	1pm to 5pm

Closed Good Friday and 18-31 December.
Last admission 4.30pm
Special opening arrangements can be made for pre-booked groups.

The ARC is a project of the York Archaeological Trust.
The Trust is a registered charity. Number 509060.

Bibliography

Primary Sources

Burdekins Almanac
Carmichael-Walker, Mabel Report of the Soldier's Home 1912 and 1930
Census for Gate Fulford 1851, 1861, 1871, 1881
Council Minutes Books 1886-1982
Electoral Rolls of Gate Fulford 1861-1982
Fulford Parish Magazine (ed. J. Erskine Clark) 1873-4, 1878-9, 1881, 1891, 1893, 1900
Map of Walmgate Stray by John Lund 1772 (Revised from George Smith's Map of 1736)
Parish Registers and Churchwarden's Accounts, Gate Fulford Parish
Ratebooks for Gate Fulford Parish 1885, 1890, 1895, 1900
Street Directories Kelly's, Stevens' and White's 1861-1975
Streets and Buildings Committee Minute Books 1889-1914, 1920-29
Watch Committee Minute Books 1879-86, 1886-1892, 1892-1898
York Cemetery Registers 1882, 1911
York City Library Newspaper Index
Yorkshire Evening Press
Yorkshire Gazette

Secondary Sources

Author's Association William Bentley 1908
Benson, George Taverns, Hostels and Inns of York Burdekins 1913.
Briggs, G Jubilee History of York Equitable Industrial Society Ltd Co-operative Wholesale Society. 1909.
Caine, Caesar Martial Annals of York C J Clark 1893.
Camidge, William Ouse Bridge to Naburn Lock 1888.
Cooper, T P The Old Inns and Inn Signs of York Delittle & Sons. 1897.
Finnegan, Frances Poverty and Prostitution : A Study of Victorian Prostitutes in York Cambridge University Press 1979
Hutchinson, J & Palliser, D M (Eds) Bartholomew Guide to York Bartholomew 1980
Knight, C B History of the City of York AD 71-1901 Herald Printers 1944
Murray, Hugh Horse Tramways of York 1880-1909 Light Rail Transit Association 1980
Murray, Hugh Pedigrees of York Families
Phillips, Margaret Mann Within the City Wall Hodder 1943
Pickering, J & Briddon, I History of Fulford Privately published
Pugh, R B (Ed.) Victoria County History: A History of Yorkshire (East Riding) Vol. 3 University of London Institute of Historical Research 1976
Royal Commission on Historical Monuments City of York Vol IV: Outside the City Walls. East of the Ouse HMSO 1975
Stephen, Leslie (Ed.) Dictionary of National Biography Vol. VIII Smith, Elder & Co. 1885
Willis, Ronald Portrait of York Robert Hale 1972
York Archaeological Trust Interim Vol. 11, No. 4 1986; Vol. 12, No. 2 1987; Vol. 13, Nos. 2 & 4 1988; Vol. 14, No. 3 1989
York Committee for the Welfare of British Asians from Uganda Green for Come Photocopied Report 1973